TWAYNE'S WORLD AUTHORS SERIES

A Survey of the World's Literature

DENMARK

Leif Sjöberg, State University of
New York at Stony Brook

EDITOR

Hans Christian Andersen

TWAS 612

Hans Christian Anderson

HANS CHRISTIAN ANDERSEN

By BO GRØNBECH

TWAYNE PUBLISHERS

A DIVISION OF G. K. HALL & CO., BOSTON

Library of Congress Cataloging in Publication Data
Grønbech, Bo.
Hans Christian Andersen.
(Twayne's world authors series; TWAS 612: Denmark)
Bibliography: p. 161–67
Includes index.
1. Andersen, Hans Christian, 1805–1875.
2. Authors, Danish—19th century—Biography.
PT8120.G74   839.8:136   80-13621
ISBN 0-8057-6454-2

This book is dedicated to P. M. Mitchell,
Professor of Germanic Languages, Urbana, Illinois,
who with untiring enthusiasm through many years
has worked to create an interest for Denmark
and Danish literature in the United States

Contents

About the Author

Bo Grønbech, who is currently president of the Hans Christian Andersen Society in Copenhagen, Denmark, was born in the Danish capital in 1907. He studied at the University of Copenhagen where he received an M.A. in 1932 and a Ph.D. (with a dissertation on Hans Christian Andersen's fairy-tale world) in 1945. From 1930 to 1977 he taught literature and history at a Copenhagen Gymnasium. Dr. Grønbech is a well-known lecturer on literary and historic subjects all over Scandinavia. In 1962. he was a visiting professor at Reed College, Oregon, and in 1975 he made an extensive lecture tour of German universities.

He is the author of two books on Hans Christian Andersen: *H. C. Andersens Eventyrverden* (1945), and *H. C. Andersen, levnedsløb—digtning—personlighed* (*H. C. Andersen—career—works—personality*, 1971). Other books include *Den græske skulpturs ansigter* (*The faces of Greek sculpture*, 1942), *Etruskerne* (*The Etruscans*, 1956), *Sicilien* (*Sicily*, 1960; abridged version, 1975), and translations into Danish of Caesar's *Gallic Wars* (1966) and Plato's *Socrates' Apology* (1974). Dr. Grønbech is a member of several learned societies and is a respected reviewer and critic in his native Copenhagen.

Preface

The aim of the present book is to give a description of Hans Christian Andersen and of his works. Scarcely any Scandinavian writer has had a career as extraordinary and a personality as fascinating as he, and he is the only Danish poet who has acquired world-wide fame. He left behind him a richly varied production, above all the fairy tales, which have spread all over the world.

The first chapter of this book is an account of his life, given at some length because his manifold experiences furnished the material of his works, to which, consequently, his life in many cases can be regarded as a commentary. As a conclusion some pages give a picture of his strange and in many respects mysterious personality. The second chapter is a presentation of his works (except the fairy tales), with a more thorough discussion of certain books. In the third chapter the intention of the author has been through an interpretation of a number of fairy tales to elucidate their character so as to promote a deeper understanding of Andersen's specific literary form—to open, so to speak, the doors to Andersen's fairy-tale universe. The fourth chapter consists of three shorter divisions: the first deals with the reception given by the reading public and the critics to Andersen's works in Denmark, Germany, England, and the United States; the second examines Andersen's influence; the third is concerned with Andersen studies in the twentieth century. The fifth chapter outlines what of Andersen's world the visitor can find in modern Denmark.

The author has endeavored to provide a scholarly description in a form comprehensible even to those who are not literary specialists.

Bo Grønbech

Acknowledgments

With the publication of this book I would like to express my respectful gratitude to the Danish State Humanistic Research Board for their considerable contribution toward the translation expenses. Furthermore, I wish to thank the Odense Municipal Museum for permission to use R. P. Keigwin's translations of poems by Andersen, and also the Danish Royal Library in Copenhagen for allowing me to make use of the photograph of Hans Christian Andersen.

Moreover, I would like to make known my indebtedness to past and present Andersen scholars, among the latter Dr. Erik Dal, the administrator of the Danish Language and Literature Society, to whom I extend my heartfelt thanks for much constructive advice in the course of the preparation of this work, and also to Niels Birger Wamberg, who in friendship read and criticized my manuscript. Of past scholars I am anxious to commemorate the late Dr. Helge Topsøe-Jensen to whom I am sincerely indebted for advice, encouragement, and friendship over many years.

Finally, my thanks to Mrs. Della Thomas, associate professor of library science, Stillwater, Oklahoma, whose earnest requests, that knowledge of Hans Christian Andersen be made available to the American public, have proved an inspiration for the completion of this study.

Chronology

1872
1862–   Journey to Spain.
1863
1866   Journey to Portugal.
1870   *Lykke-Peer* (*Lucky Peer*).
1873   Last journey (to Switzerland).
1875   2 April, celebrates seventieth birthday. 4 August, dies in the
          Melchior's home. 11 August, funeral held in Copenhagen's
          cathedral.

CHAPTER 1

The Life of Hans Christian Andersen

I *Childhood*

A. Poverty and genius

ONE hundred and seventy-five years ago there was no such thing as a welfare state in Denmark. Very few people were as well-off as most are today, and poverty was far too common. Social benefits were few and the poor had to make do as best they could. Often they had to live literally on scraps from the tables of the wealthy. In the country and in small towns the poor often went out at harvest time and gleaned stray ears of corn just as Ruth did in the harvest fields of the wealthy Boaz. So one day in August 1810 or 1811 a group of women went into the fields outside the small Danish town of Odense; one of them had her young son with her to help. Care was necessary for they knew that on the nearby farm there was a bullying bailiff who usually chased them away if he discovered them. On this August day he caught them by surprise. Suddenly there he was with a large dog whip in his hand. They all started running to get away, but the little boy could not keep up, the bailiff overtook him and lifted his whip to strike. Then the boy turned, looked him straight in the eyes, and said. "How dare you strike me when you know that God is watching you!" The bailiff lowered his whip, stood a moment, patted the boy's cheek, asked him his name, gave him a few farthings, and then let him run on. When he showed them to his mother, she said to the other women, "He's a strange boy, my Hans Christian, everybody is kind to him, and even the bad bailiff has given him money." [1]

That boy was Hans Christian Andersen, later to become famous for his fairy tales. In his story about the ugly duckling the baby swan is hatched out in a duck's nest and grows up in a duck yard, but there is no explanation as to how the swan's egg came to be among the duck's. Nor can anyone explain why the poor shoemaker from Odense should have a genius as a son. That he was born with an unusual personality is obvious from the episode with the bailiff. That he possessed unique talent as a writer was to be apparent in time.

B. Odense

Denmark lies between the North Sea and the Baltic, protected on one side by Sweden and on the other by the broad back of Jutland. In between lies a multitude of islands big and small. The largest is Zealand with the capital Copenhagen on the far east side of the sound and facing Sweden. The second largest island is Funen, which lies protected under the east coast of Jutland. Odense is the largest city on the island and fourth largest in Denmark. Today about 165,000 people live there. Residential housing sectors have now spread right around the city. In the city center the streets still wind as they have done for centuries, but new and ultramodern buildings have replaced the beautiful old houses, though fortunately a few of them still exist here and there.

Back in the nineteenth century Odense was also the fourth largest town in Denmark though with a much smaller population of scarcely 7,000 people, which for those times was a considerable number. Odense was what people in Denmark at that time called an important town. Furthermore, a bishop had his seat there. The Gothic cathedral, St. Canute's, towered above the city, and its spire could be seen both then and now from afar. The cathedral faced the marketplace, as did the medieval town hall and the grammar school. Just to the south was the little river that formed the town boundary, and beyond it lay the open country. The north side of the marketplace ran into the main street and farther away was the theater where traveling theatrical companies or actors from the Royal Theater in Copenhagen would perform, and the still extant Odense Castle, an elegant edifice set back in delightful grounds, from 1816 the residence of Prince Christian Frederik, who later became King Christian VIII. It was the fashionable world that gave the town its air of distinction: the nobility, army officers, civil servants, merchants, and rich artisans. They lived in fine well-kept houses, promenaded along the main street, held dances and costumed balls, attended the concerts and the theater.

Alongside this wealthy class, yet sharply separated from it, lived those who were not so well off. These were the common people scarcely living from hand to mouth. They lived in the narrow side streets packed together in low houses. Today a walk down Hans

Jensenstræde to the Hans Christian Andersen Museum gives an impression of what these houses were like.

This segment of the community was surprisingly large. It would seem that about one half of the town's population was what was termed "poor." That is to say they lived from casual labor or public support. Among them were day laborers and soldiers, as well as many single women who supported themselves, wretchedly of course, by spinning, sewing, and washing for other people.

A not inconsiderable proportion of the large artisan class was to be counted among the "poor," viz., the so-called free masters who were not admitted as members of the guilds and so not entitled to train an apprentice. Socially they ranked as day laborers, and though at times they lived better than these, their circumstances were still often straitened. It was into the family of such a free master that Denmark's famous writer was born in the year of 1805.

His father, Hans Andersen, was a shoemaker. Hans Christian Andersen relates that his grandparents had been well-to-do farmers, but had suffered misfortunes, and in 1788 had moved to Odense where they lived in poverty. The latter information is correct, the former certainly not. The grandfather probably was a shoemaker like his son[3] and moreover had become insane and wandered the streets of Odense, a mad eccentric, the laughing stock of the street urchins.

Hans Christian Andersen in his autobiographies makes no mention of his mother's relatives, and if he did know anything he had no wish to publicize it. The one thing he mentions about her childhood was that she had once been forced out to beg, and since nobody took pity on her she sat weeping the whole day under a bridge. Certainly, her family lived in poverty. Her mother probably came from the country west of Odense. Recent research has traced part of her life. It would seem that she was born about 1745 and had no fewer than three illegitimate daughters before she was married in Odense in 1783 to a tailor, who had just been released from prison.[4]

The eldest of these three daughters was Hans Christian Andersen's mother who was born early in the 1770s. The second daughter, born in 1778, went to Copenhagen in 1799, where Hans Christian Andersen eventually visited her; but only once, for she was living in a brothel. Nothing is known about the third daughter.

There are obvious reasons why Hans Christian Andersen had no wish to record this piece of family history in his official memoirs and why he remained silent about his mother's background. She probably

spent several years in service with various families in Odense and in
1799 gave birth to an illegitimate daughter. Hans Christian
Andersen's half-sister grew up in Odense and later moved to
Copenhagen. For many years he dreaded her seeking him out. He
could not help her; moreover, he had been accepted into much
higher circles than the one they had both come from. His diaries
reveal that she visited him just once (in 1842). It is now known that
she died in 1846.[5]

Considering the unsatisfactory social conditions it is commendable
that Hans Christian Andersen's parents were able to provide a relatively secure childhood home and that he himself was able to lead
what was considered in those days a correct, though unusual, and
respectable life.

Indeed, the only irregularity in his life was the timing of his birth
just two months after his parents' wedding. In his famous autobiography, *The Story of My Life*, he gives a charming description of that day
in 1805—2 April—when he came into the world. If this is read in
conjunction with the description of his home, which immediately
follows it, one is left with the impression that he was born in the house
where he spent his childhood. This cannot be so, however. Where
Hans Christian Andersen was born is not known, only that after his
parents' marriage on 2 February 1805 they were not able to live
together until early in 1806.[6] In May 1807 they settled in the lower
part of the marketplace in what is now called Munkemøllestræde,
which then as now led down to the river. The humble half-timbered
house with its little garden, really no more than a yard, is still there.

Several families lived in the house; there were at least six in 1809,
so the shoemaker and his family had no more than a single room. This
is the room so touchingly described in *The Story of My Life*.[7] His
parents were rather ill matched. He was twenty-two years old and she
at least thirty when they married. He was small, fair haired, and had a
round face; she was big and strong, dark of skin, and had brown eyes.
Their dispositions, too, were quite different. He appears to have
been fairly intelligent and would like to have studied had not his
parents' poverty forced him to become a shoemaker. He never seems
to have forgotten this disappointment. In his spare time he comforted
himself by reading such things as the comedies of Holberg (1684–
1754), the greatest Danish dramatist; but he could scarcely have been
satisfied with his situation and was capable of being ill tempered and
moody.

The shoemaker's wife was a striking contrast. With her, wrote her son, "the heart was everything." [8] She was practical and frank, took irreproachable care of her husband and child, and conscientiously kept house. [9]

Although they were such a contrast they lived harmoniously together, and Hans Christian noticed no serious conflicts—at least, not in the first years. His father was devoted to him, took him walking in the woods, made a theater and other toys for him, and, of an evening, read aloud from Holberg, La Fontaine, and *The Arabian Nights*.

Many of his most significant childhood experiences were gained through his paternal grandmother. She earned a little money by tending to the porter's garden at the old people's asylum known as Greyfriars Hospital. Hans Christian often accompanied her, and it was there that he heard the old women in the spinning room tell legends and folktales. Beyond this, there was little variety in his everyday save a visit to the local theater, which, of course, was a place of entertainment for people of quality; the less fortunate could afford the price of admission only once a year.

Andersen's autobiographies leave the impression that his childhood was a happy period. His parents loved each other and him. Yet this idyll can hardly have lasted very many years. His father grew increasingly discontented with his situation. He became depressed, his son wrote, and his restlessness increased until he enlisted in the King's Regiment. [10] In 1807 Denmark had been drawn into the Napoleonic Wars on the side of Napoleon. Danish troops had to march to Germany as allies. The shoemaker greatly admired Napoleon, and he hoped to have the opportunity to fight for his hero and perhaps return as an officer. His regiment did not, however, get further than Holstein and was never involved in any fighting. Peace was declared in January 1814, and the shoemaker returned home having achieved nothing but to ruin his health. He only lived two more years and died, a broken man, on 26 April 1816, shortly after his son's eleventh birthday. "The Ice Maiden has taken him," said Hans Christian's mother sadly, and he remembered how the previous winter his father had shown him frost patterns on the window panes resembling a maid stretching out both her arms. "She's come to fetch me," his father had said in jest. The jest had turned into merciless reality. [11]

From now on his mother had to keep the home going alone; though in fact she had been doing so ever since her husband left Odense in 1813. In the same year need had been brought to many homes throughout the country, which was in an economic crisis because of the war. His mother worked hard to earn their keep; she even stood in the river to wash clothes, a tough job sufficient to turn even a strong woman to drink, which she eventually did.

Understandably, her son was left even more to himself. He played with the toys his father had made, particularly the theater, and read. Perhaps he was still attending school at this time, though there is no definite evidence. He was an apt pupil, learned quickly by heart, and never needed to do his homework. At school he cut a strange figure. He sat daydreaming during lessons and sometimes tried to share his own strange stories with the other children. But he soon stopped trying, for they said he was not right in the head, "mad, like his grandfather," [12] a comment that filled him with horror—suppose it were true! So he kept mainly to himself and took no part in their games. Nevertheless, he seemed to get on well with them, was never involved in fights, and was much a teacher's favorite.

By this time Hans Christian Andersen was lanky, had thick fair hair, and with his long nose and small eyes presented a remarkable spectacle. Peculiar he was, but not without attraction, and he possessed a strangely naive and frank forwardness that gradually won him important acquaintances even high up in society. Reading was his favorite occupation. As soon as he heard of someone having books he would introduce himself. His naive openness took them by surprise, and he was soon borrowing books from everyone in the neighborhood. But he progressed beyond these acquaintances. It is not clear from his autobiographies how it came about but he was soon known by prominent people in Odense as a singer and as a reciter of Holberg. He performed in the house of the city pharmacist and of the bishop, where Colonel Høegh-Guldberg took notice of him, and very soon he reached the peak of Odense society when he was brought before Prince Christian at Odense Castle. [13]

It must have been Høegh-Guldberg who drew Prince Christian's attention to the boy. The prince expressed the desire to see him, and when Andersen was presented he was advised that if the prince were to enquire of his ambitions he should reply that he wished to study. This first encounter between his royal highness and this strange child of the people was to pass in a typical Andersen manner. He acted some Holberg, sang an improvised song, and then the prince asked whether he wanted to become an actor. With his usual forthrightness he replied that he did, but naively added that he had been told to say that he wished to study. This did not go down well, and the prince reminded him that he was a child from a poor family and would do better to learn a suitable trade, such as wood turning. "If you agree, let me know and I will consider the matter." Whereupon the audience was over.[14] They were not to know that their next meeting was to be under quite different circumstances.

Andersen was by no means content with the prospect of becoming a turner. He continued playing and, most of all, reading—the Bible, Shakespeare, Holberg and other Danish dramatists, novels from the lending library, and much else. A little later he started writing tragedies where all the characters, as they ought, died. To all who would listen he read his own works and was soon known for doing so. In fact, on one occasion the street urchins followed him, howling, "There goes the play scribbler." The young writer fled home to hide himself in a corner and pray to God.[15]

C. Departure from Odense

At Easter 1819 he was confirmed in the cathedral, and now a decision had to be taken about his future. The suggestion of a trade again came up. Confronted with this prospect the appalled boy protested, wept, and pleaded. He wanted to be an actor, not an artisan. Accordingly, he left Odense for Copenhagen, with the hope of becoming an actor.

Various circumstances had long prepared him for this decision. As a child he had already acquired a love for the theater which had turned to a passion the previous year when Odense had been visited by a troupe of actors and singers from the Royal Theater in Copenhagen. Their performances had made such a strong impression on him that he could not doubt that his life lay in the theater.

The real force behind his reckless decision, however, lay deeper than his passion for the theater. What he probably did not realize was that the compulsion driving him forward was the desire to escape: to escape from the restricting environment of Odense to a wider world where there was room for his expansive, explosive temperament. His potential was too great. Instinctively he must have realized that to remain in his native town would have meant spiritual suffocation. Would his family and neighbors understand? Certainly not. Neither did he. But he could not be budged from his resolution. He told his mother that he had read of unusual famous men of humble origin: "First you go through terrible suffering, and then you become famous."[16] He reminded her of his father's dictum that he should never be forced to do anything he did not want to and that she herself had let an old woman tell his fortune. Glaring at him, the old woman had said, "He will have better luck than he deserves. He will be a wild bird, flying high up and being grand. One day the town of Odense will be illuminated in his honor." [17] His mother had been delighted at that time, but now that the leap forward was to be made she found the prophecy being used against her own arguments.

In the end his mother gave in. He was so full of optimism. In fairy tales and comedies all ended well, and certainly God would not let him down. It was unfortunate not to know a single soul in the vastness of Copenhagen, and everybody advised him to carry a letter of introduction, but who could supply one? Guldberg was away, and the prince could not be imposed upon. So he prevailed upon the local printer, Mr. Iversen, who had had contact with the royal actors in the previous year, to give him an introduction to Madame Schall, the prima ballerina of the Royal Theater. [18] With this letter, and his savings of fourteen rigsdaler, in his pocket and a little bundle of clothes in his hand, he took leave of his mother and his grandmother. He had to go by the mail coach as an unofficial passenger. He left on 4 September 1819. The great journey into the unknown had begun.

II   Youth[19]

From Odense to the capital was a journey that involved crossing the Great Belt by sailing boat to the small port of Korsør and then a thirty-six-hour coach ride across the island of Zealand. While standing on deck watching the coastline of his home island fade away Andersen felt oppressed; but when he arrived in Korsør he went behind a shed, fell on his knees in prayer to God, and wept. Thus relieved, his courage returned, and he happily continued on his mail-coach journey to Copenhagen.

Early in the morning of 6 September he was dropped on Frederiks-berg Hill on the outskirts of Copenhagen, for being an unofficial passenger, he could not accompany the coach into the city. On the hill is an early eighteenth-century castle which at that time was the king's summer residence. Below the castle lies one of Copenhagen's most attractive parks. Nowadays the city has spread around the castle and its park, but in those days fields, gardens, and small houses could be seen from the hilltop, while in the background were the beautiful towers for which the capital was already famous. It was this view that the young boy now had before him that Monday morning. The

Promised Land! He burst into tears and felt that now he had no one to help him save God in his Heaven. He hitched up his bundle of clothes and walked on toward the object of his desires. After a little more than half an hour he arrived in the city. Just inside the city gate he took up lodgings at 18 Vestergade, a house that still exists.

By European standards the capital of Denmark was then a small city with narrow, winding streets and attractive houses, most of them from the eighteenth century. Major disasters had visited Copenhagen: first there was the great fire in 1728 when more than half of the houses were burned to ashes, then came the bombardment in 1807 when the English, after Denmark's unfortunate entry into the Napoleonic Wars, had rained fire and explosive bombs upon the city for three days. Even in 1819 there were gaps in the rows of houses, particularly in the western part of the city where Hans Christian Andersen had taken up lodgings. But he hardly noticed them when, immediately after his arrival, he hurried off in search of the Royal Theatre.

A. The Theater

This theater was founded in 1748 by King Frederik V as the home not only of drama but also of opera and ballet. It was sited near the harbor on what is now an open space between Magasin du Nord, a departmental store, and the present theater building, which was erected in 1874. As might be expected his heart was beating wildly when he found himself standing outside the object of his childhood dreams, and he prayed that he would soon be inside and become a good actor.

On the following day he commenced his efforts to gain entrance to the theatre world. Wearing his brown confirmation clothes and clutching his letter of introduction, he called on Madame Schall, the solo dancer.[20] She must have been amazed to see the strange, long figure and to hear him tell of his wish to join the theater. She asked him to show what he could do, and so he recited, danced, and sang for his astonished audience, who, of course, could not promise him anything but only refer him to the director of the theater. However, his reception there produced no better a result.[21]

But Andersen did not give up. With the incredible ability to acquire friends he managed, via them, to meet others of the theater's artists who gave him the opportunity to try his fortune, first as a ballet dancer and later as a singer in the opera choir. Other kindly disposed people helped him financially, and so it was possible for him to keep going for three years—a period full of contradictions. He scraped and starved his way, lived in a miserable room in one of the most disreputable districts of Copenhagen, but made acquaintances and friends among the most prominent members of society such as Oehlenschläger and Ingemann, both poets of great reputation, and the famous H. C. Ørsted (1777–1851), the discoverer of electromagnetism; they all took a liking to the strange boy from the provinces with his open, friendly manner and his great love for poetry and the theater.

But all of no avail. After three years the theater management dismissed him from further service.[22]

B. Conclusion of the Copenhagen Years

His hazardous flirtation with the theater had been brought to an end. Three hard years had passed. He had lived under humble, even wretched, circumstances. He had attended ballet school and the opera's choir school, had received occasional lessons in recitation from an actor—but all this had led to nothing. Those three years were wasted, or so it seemed. But really they were not. He had learned much more than he realized. He seems to have attended the theater practically every evening, and there he gained an awareness of current tastes in drama. Many of the plays that had called forth cheers and tears have long since been forgotten, though, of course, the classics were also performed and Andersen saw them too: the comedies of Holberg, Oehlenschläger's tragedies, plays by Schiller and Lessing and one of Molière, Mozart's operas, musical comedies by Méhul, Cherubini, and Rossini (who at this time was acquiring a name in Copenhagen).

In addition to theatergoing, Hans Christian Andersen was avidly reading books and literary periodicals, so it is understandable that in the course of those years he had little difficulty in attaining a degree of culture comparable with that of any educated Copenhagener. The theater also taught him one more essential thing—bearing—an acquisition that later in life meant he was able to move in the courts of Europe as though to the manner born. This deportment was largely due to the training he received at the ballet school and to watching, evening after evening, the many distinguished performers on the stage.

Those years also prepared him for the future in other ways. He was becoming conscious of the extremes of Danish society. His childhood was among the poor, and in Copenhagen he experienced the misery of the urban masses. There was prostitution around him even if he dared not, or did not want to, understand what was going on. Yet even while living in these disreputable surroundings, he established contacts with artists and scientists who were to play their parts later as friends and benefactors. Seven years later, when his first works were published, he was already at ease among the most distinguished representatives of Danish culture.

The value of these experiences and acquaintances were, of course, unknown to him when he stood with the theater's dismissal in his hand early in the summer of 1822. Everything seemed hopeless. Should he give up? Certainly not, first, because there was no other way than to continue; second, because he could not bring himself to abandon the theater; and finally, there was still another chance—if he could not become an actor then perhaps he could be a playwright and write tragedies like Oehlenschläger and other famous writers.[23] Immediately he commenced a fresh assault on the temple of art that he had been attacking in vain for so long.

As a child in Odense he had tried writing plays, and so once more he tried again. Soon a drama was finished, and he delivered it to the theater. It came back at once. So he wrote one more and this caused the theater's literary consultant, K. L. Rahbek, to lift his eyebrows in surprise. True, the play was quite immature nonsense, full of un-digested romantic clichés; Rahbek clutched his head in despair over the language and the spelling. Nevertheless, being an experienced man of letters, Rahbek read on carefully and he observed that beneath the many immature tirades a natural talent lay buried; perhaps something might come out from "this curious head," [24] as he wrote in his criticism. Therefore, he earnestly recommended his three colleagues on the board of directors to assist in appealing for royal support for the young person in order that "his unmistakable talent could be developed and cultivated."

The three others agreed and Andersen was called before the board on 13 September 1822.[25] It must have been with considerable trepidation that the ambitious young writer approached the theater. Would they accept his play for performance? Would they recognize him as the great new hope of Danish literature? Neither of these things happened. The board was assembled, and Rahbek, as spokesman, announced that the submitted work showed the author's complete lack of education; but he added that there were signs in it that promised well for the future. Moreover, since the author appeared to be an unspoiled young person an appeal would be submitted to the king for a royal grant to enable Andersen to attend a grammar school. Jonas Collin, a senior government official and one of the directors of the theater, was to take whatever measures were necessary, and Andersen was to refer to him from now on.

The youth was speechless with joy. He was saved! The thought of having to attend school was perhaps at the moment not so attractive, but this meant little compared with the fact that from now on the desperate and exhausting struggle to keep body and soul together was over. From now on he was certain for a few years of having a roof over his head and food every day; he could look forward to a secure and orderly existence that would provide the possibility for him to create a future—a far greater possibility than he had had at the theater where his prospects had never been promising.

Matters were settled rapidly. Collin arranged for him to have free tuition at the grammar school in Slagelse (a small town fifty-six miles west of Copenhagen) together with an annual grant for the duration of his studies. On the 26 October he took the coach to Slagelse to begin a new and, as it proved, both useful and troublesome phase in his development.

As a fourteen-year-old, Hans Christian Andersen had arrived in Copenhagen not knowing a single person there and without having the capability of earning enough even for the simple necessities of life. He survived for three years solely on help from people who had taken an interest in him. Finally, when everything had gone wrong and he had reached rock bottom, he had practically forced public assistance onto himself: the hand of God or destiny? The explanation lies in the man: his strange appearance, his stubborn faith in his talent, his perseverance, and that powerful personal magnetism that nobody could escape. Nobody could resist his intensely good-natured entreating eyes, or hold off his naive insistency that would not be stopped for any consideration whatsoever: he so greatly needed a helping hand, for it was a matter of life or death, and he possessed the genius' unreflecting conviction that he deserved to be helped and that Denmark would gain by his being helped. It was impossible to refuse him.

But despite these reasonable explanations of his benefactors' interest in him, it must be admitted that he had had remarkably good fortune, and that he might so easily have gone to the dogs. He had every reason to thank providence for his salvation.

C. School [26]

Jonas Collin (1776–1861), renowned for his competence and up-rightness, was one of the senior civil servants in whom King Frederik VI (King 1808–1839) had most confidence. He was a director of the treasury and adviser to the king on all sorts of administrative and cultural problems, an extremely busy man, who nevertheless still found time for those who needed his advice and assistance. He had immediately perceived that Hans Christian Andersen was of a quality deserving to be helped and took on the administration of the fund that the king had provided. Furthermore, Collin took it upon himself to keep an eye on Andersen's progress, and from the very beginning threw his house open to him and became a parental guide and friend to the fatherless youth.

The responsibility for his daily tuition was placed in the hands of the headmaster in Slagelse, a short, stout man named Simon Meis-ling, who received him kindly and invited him to spend the first evening at his house. Andersen immediately read aloud from his own writings, including the rejected plays. This was a somewhat brash opening to their relationship, but then Andersen never stopped to reflect whenever he was engrossed by something, and was there anything more interesting in all the world than his own poetry?

However, the following morning, 28 October 1822, his prosaic schooling commenced. The seventeen-year-old Hans Christian was placed in a class among pupils who were five or six years younger than he, and above them his lanky figure towered. It might be expected that the boys would tease their strange new companion but this did not happen. From the very start they respected him and quite soon came to appreciate his friendly nature. He also got on well with his teachers. However, even his elementary knowledge was practically nonexistent and so he had great difficulties in keeping pace with the others, who had, after all, numerous years of regular schooling be-hind them. Keeping his head up became an inhuman drudgery. But this was not the worst problem confronting him.

The real trouble came from his headmaster and mentor who had received him so kindly that first day but who had soon changed direction. Meisling was a distinguished philologist and a high-principled educationalist, well-known for his severity and thorough-ness, but he had little understanding of young people and absolutely none of his exceptional pupil. With his fiery and unpredictable tem-perament, he became inordinately irritated by Andersen's lack of knowledge and study routine, constantly showing his anger and vexation in an utterly ruthless manner. Andersen worked incredibly hard and with time achieved respectable results in most subjects, but he had always to be prepared for all sorts of mockery and indignities, and so it went on year after year. For such a hypersensitive soul this state of affairs must have turned his schooldays into one long martyr-dom. That he was able to survive was due to that strange tenacity he always displayed during times of adversity. This tenacity was re-flected in his belief that God could not fail him. There was also his consideration for his benefactors, whom he did not want to dis-appoint, particularly Jonas Collin, in whom he regularly confided about his studies and all the fears that beset him—fear of his headmas-ter's caprices and fear of not being good enough—and whose possible anger he sought to allay.

Behind all these worries lay, however, a deep-rooted feeling of not being mature enough to respond to the demands of an adult world. "My childish nature is still with me yet I feel so content with it," was how Andersen put it in a letter to an elderly lady in Copenhagen in 1823.[27] This would seem to indicate that he still had a child's spon-taneity to experiences and reactions, which, regrettably, was ex-tremely impractical in his present situation. He was constantly hav-ing to pull himself together in order to face the reality of his existence with the necessary determination. This immediacy, or softness of spirit as he himself put it, was one of the secrets of his personality, and in time was to prove to be his strength. Yet this was closely linked with an innate nervous frailty, which now, and throughout his life, caused him great suffering, and manifested itself in recurrent de-pressions.

In 1825 Meisling was appointed headmaster of the grammar school at Elsinore, a town on the northeast point of Zealand where—accord-ing to tradition—Hamlet had once lived. But the cheerfulness of that old seaport was not for Andersen. Meisling kept him at his books and bullied him more than ever. Collin finally realized how bad things were and in 1827 concluded that Andersen should move to Copenhagen, where a young theologian by the name of Ludvig Müller was willing to act as his tutor and prepare him for his examen artium in his final year.[28]

He had learned a great deal in school (as one did in those days): Latin, Greek, Hebrew, French, history, mathematics, and religion, but not so much the self-discipline, order, concentration, and thor-oughness that his headmaster had tried to impart. Andersen was a bohemian by nature, and his nervous system could not tolerate the harshness that Meisling had meted out. Therefore, he probably learned most from his private tutor who was of a cheerful disposition and treated his pupil with a warmth which was the only climate in which Hans Christian Andersen could thrive. In October 1828 Andersen passed his examen artium.

III *First Creations*

A. A New Life [29]

For a boy of humble origin such as Andersen it was an achievement to have come so far. Social equality, first proclaimed as part of a political manifesto in 1776 in the American Declaration of Independence and which, theoretically, the democracies of the West now approve and in practice are then attempting to realize, did not exist in contemporary Denmark, just as it did not in other European societies, and nobody dreamed of introducing it. Danish society was comprised of two distinct layers—the upper layer was made up of the nobility and the relatively wealthy while the lower level consisted of the great mass of humble people: in the country, all the small farmers and laborers; in the town, the artisans, small tradespeople, workers, and the rest of the proletariat. To climb up from the lower to the upper layer was not a simple task. In Odense Prince Christian had reminded Andersen, when he was a boy, that he was of humble origin and should not think of more than learning an attractive trade. In other words: where you are, you stay. The circumstances would have to be quite exceptional for a child of low birth to break through this class barrier. Few were capable of the effort. Andersen was one of the few: he would and he could.

His examen artium was proof that he had a right to a place in the sun, and he was contented with his new life. He took up lodging in a small garret in Vingårdsstræde near the Royal Theater (the house is now owned by Magasin du Nord and the garret today looks as it did then), not far from his many friends, all those he had made during his three years with the theater, and whom he was now able to visit as often as he wished. This meant dinner and pleasant company. It is true, though, that in return he had to undergo a number of admonitions and similar attempts to improve his upbringing: far too many in his opinion, and he never learned to understand the value of them. There is the possibility that they did help to limit his self-absorption somewhat and thereby helped him to a degree of adjustment to the society of Copenhagen. His "improvers" meant well and probably feared that he would develop into a conceited fellow.

Many prominent people in the cultural world opened their houses to him, but his real home was at Jonas Collin's where he was regarded and treated as a son. Here developed a cheerful and highly special family life, much influenced by the five grown-up children.[30] As true Copenhageners they were skeptical and rarely impressed, not even by Andersen's great ambitions or the world-wide reputation he gradually acquired (the cat-and-hen scene in *The Ugly Duckling* indicates how the family's egocentricity affected Andersen). Despite all his peculiarities—his self-centeredness and his touchiness—they were very fond of him, and the friendship was mutual. Edvard Collin, the second son, became Andersen's closest friend. He was three years younger than Andersen but because of his greater personal stability appeared older. He took his law exams and entered the civil service like his father. Edvard Collin was a very undemonstrative young man, far more level-headed than Andersen would have liked, but he was unflaggingly helpful. During Andersen's schooling he helped him with his Latin exercises and, later on, he became his adviser on all sorts of matters, both practical and personal. Because of the great difference in temperament, disagreements between them were not unusual, particularly in their younger years, for example, in 1831 when the reserved Edvard Collin declined, for a number of reasons, to use the familiar "du" form of address, preferring to remain on more formal terms in his relationship with Andersen. Fifteen years later Andersen used the episode in his tale *The Shadow*, though in another and more universal perspective. Yet despite all difficulties their friendship lasted a lifetime.

One year after passing his examen artium Andersen successfully took the examination in philosophy and philology that all students at Copenhagen University had to pass before they could proceed with their specialized studies. But should he study? No, he was just not suited. He felt that his calling was to be a poet and old Jonas Collin helped confirm this, "Now, follow the path you are probably created for," he said, "it will most likely be the best." [31]

B. The Literary Environment

Thus he was now about to try to earn a living as a writer, an undertaking that in Denmark both then and now was certainly not easy. Not one of his fellow artists could make ends meet from writing alone. They all had some sort of post or profession. Andersen was different. He embarked upon a highly uncertain course. He could not rely on any regular income, and he had to live without that moral support the others had from being aware that they were useful members of society: it was a make or break situation. If he could not become a great poet or writer and thereby hold his own, then he was nothing. But this was his only chance. He was quite unsuited for anything else than being a poet. In this light his hectic race to publish throughout the subsequent years was understandable. He had to earn a living and, no matter the cost, he had to make a name for himself in the world of literature. He had to prove to himself and those around him that he, a child of humble origin, was just as good a writer as all those others, who were born in the upper layer.

It is worth the while to stop here for a moment to consider the class into which he was now entering. During the eighteenth century Denmark had become part of the European cultural society. Renaissance ideas had been introduced by the towering figure of Ludvig Holberg, the founder of Danish literature. His works on European and Danish history, written for the general public and throughout the subsequent century widely read, his satirical poetry, and, above all, his comedies, written in the 1720s, came to form the foundation of Danish literature and Danish thought. He formulated the ideas of rationalism that for the rest of the eighteenth century dominated Danish intellectual life. His comedies were performed at the Royal Theatre, and continue to be presented to this day.

By the turn of the century, however, other ideas were asserting themselves. In 1802 a gifted twenty-nine-year-old philosopher and scientist by the name of Henrik Steffens visited Denmark. Born in Norway, which at that time was part of the Danish realm, he was a cousin of Grundtvig (who later became Denmark's greatest hymn writer and also the founder of the Danish folk high school movement). He had studied in Germany where he had assimilated the ideas of romanticism. These ideas he brought to Denmark through his lectures in Copenhagen in 1802, and by so doing gave impetus to Danish romanticism, which though inspired by the German writers and poets was genuinely Danish in its form. Consequently a new poetry arose seeking its subject matter preferably in Germanic antiquity and the Middle Ages (those barbaric times as the eighteenth-century rationalists had put it), and which valued emotions higher than reason or, in other words, content higher than form.

Steffens's first adept was the young Adam Oehlenschläger (1779–1850), who with the intuition of a genius seized this new literary manifesto and within a few years had created a Danish school of romantic writings (above all, lyric and drama), which was to become a gospel for a whole new generation of Danish writers and poets. But Steffens also brought from Germany a new philosophy concerning the position of poetry and the poet in society: the spiritual world versus materialism; a conflict that had always existed in Christian Europe but was accentuated by the romantics, who regarded poetry as a message from the higher spiritual world. The poets were its representatives in the temporal world. They were something more than ordinary people. Their fraternity constituted a third and uppermost rung in nineteenth-century Danish society, a rung above the aristocracy and the wealthy classes—a conception that was generally accepted in Copenhagen society in those decades. The poet-writer was regarded with considerable respect, especially if he had his works performed on the stage of the Royal Theatre, that glittering center of the world of culture, the eternal temple of art in the center of temporality.

Therefore, it was a thoroughly romantic environment into which the Hans Christian Andersen entered as a young poet. Admittedly, a counterreaction to some of the romantic ideas was under way. Johan Ludvig Heiberg (1791–1860) had never nourished that interest in antiquity and the Middle Ages, which permeates Oehlenschläger's historic plays. Heiberg wrote "singspiele" (a kind of musical comedy) where the events took place in contemporary bourgeois society. Furthermore, in contrast to certain romantics, he proclaimed the need for a well-conceived and well-executed form—poetics was not just enthusiasm and inspiration but also a craft that had to be learned by conscious work. In his opinion Denmark had far too many amateurs who believed enthusiasm alone was sufficient.

However, on one point he himself was a romantic; he also believed in the two worlds, the spiritual and social. He did not try to conceal the fact that he regarded the representatives of the spiritual world as more distinguished than the ordinary restricted member of society (philistines as the romantics, not without a certain contempt, called them).

C. First Years of Writing

It was in such literary surroundings that the young Hans Christian

Andersen was to make himself felt. He had to climb to the third and uppermost level of society, and he was well on his way. Already in 1827 and 1828 he had won the favor of the public with some minor poems, published in newspapers and periodicals, and in 1829 with the lyrical-satirical tale "Fodreise" and the comedy "Kjærlighed på Nicolai Taarn" (performed at the Royal Theater). Older, respected poets such as Oehlenschläger had shown interest and given encouragement. Even Heiberg, although he represented another taste than Oehlenschläger's, had found pleasure in Andersen's first poems. The critics, too, recognized the young man's gifts and wished to encourage him.

His production increased rapidly. In the course of the next two years he published two collections of poems, wrote the lyrics for two operas, and adapted two French plays for the Danish stage. Part of his production was performed at the Royal Theatre—the gateway to Parnassus seemed to be opening.

He soon became a well-known figure in the small world of Copenhagen. His lanky body, the loosely swinging arms, those enormous feet, and that face with its long nose and broad peasant-cheekbones were unmistakable features. He must have been aware that the Copenhageners were amused by his appearance and that they considered him ugly, but he liked to be known and recognized. He was enjoying himself and leading the kind of life that exactly suited him. He mixed with many people, often took the opportunity to read his works aloud (too often, his friends thought), and in general was regarded as one of the most promising younger writers.

His activities resulted in such an income that since his requirements were modest, he could afford to travel about in Denmark, and in 1831 even in Germany, where he established literary contacts. He would like to have paid his respects to Goethe, but he feared that this Olympic figure would be too formal and distinguished for him and so he gave up the thought of visiting the great writer, "who in my opinion is elevated most magnificently when seen, like church spires, from a distance," which was how he expressed himself in his book about the journey through Germany.[32] But he did visit Tieck, the grand old man of German romantic poetics, and Chamisso, who knew sufficient Danish to translate some of Andersen's poems, and by so doing brought Andersen's name to the attention of the German reading public, which was great encouragement for the ambitious young poet. Indeed, luck seemed to be guiding his hand.

D. Love [33]

Clouds, however, occasionally blotted the sun. During the summer of 1830, while he was traveling around the island of Funen, he arrived at the small town of Fåborg, where he was planning to meet a fellow student, Christian Voigt, the son of a wealthy local merchant and a shipowner. Their reunion was pleasurable, but more important was the fact that he met Christian's sister, Riborg Voigt, a delightful, brown-eyed girl with an attractive personality, who was a year younger than Andersen. From the very first moment they were at ease in each other's company, for she was well-read and knew his poems: there was much to talk about. For the brief period he was at Fåborg they were together each day, either at her parents' home or on excursions in the neighborhood, and their mutual understanding flourished. Very soon he realized that he was in love! Seriously in love! This is, of course, a momentous discovery for any young person, but for Andersen it immediately developed into a problem, for he felt the ground slipping beneath him. To be in love—deeply in love! He was almost panic stricken. Here were new demands on him requiring him to go beyond his private dreams and aspirations, to experiences that were foreign to his shy temperament, and which might have quite terrifying tangible consequences. To commit himself for life; his nerve failed at the thought. Engagement and marriage would mean he would have to obtain a position, some form of respectable employment, and this would mean a regulated existence, and the end to his freedom of movement. A caged bird—not a pleasant thought for a man of his bohemian nature. Less clearly did he perceive that those ordinary everyday responsibilities would prevent him from being faithful to his calling, and from obeying those impulses that crowded into his fertile mind. Perhaps he also suspected that he, with his nervous temperament, might not be able to bear intimate contact, day after day, with another person, someone who had a right to his attention and feelings.

However, this great dilemma was resolved a few months later when he met her again, this time in Copenhagen. His apprehensions overcame his love. He decided to resign her to another. A year later she married this childhood friend, and the poet was left alone with the bittersweet experience of having met love and having been made unhappy by it.

This unhappiness, nevertheless, was for him a positive experience. The disappointment sharpened his emotional life in a way that the creative artist always needs. Perhaps it should be remembered that at this period disappointed love was very much in fashion among young poets. Andersen had tasted the apple and gained a new experience; there was the satisfaction of knowing that he was "a true poet" in this respect, too. Yet the episode did move him deeply. Two of his best-known love poems, "Two brown eyes" and "The thought of my thoughts," were written during this period, and he was never to forget Riborg Voigt.

E. Criticism and Melancholy

More disappointments and difficulties were awaiting him. True, he had passed through the gateway of Parnassus but to progress further he would have to produce something weightier than those bright little verses that he had so far offered his readers. Reviewers and critics let him know that ultimately more was expected of a promising poet. They reproached him for negligence toward both poetic form and language. Worst of all, the Royal Theater had had enough of his plays, which, admittedly, did reveal the haste of his production. He was too eager to have his works performed on the stage and could not realize that his dramatic talent was not very great.

This reaction from the experts cut him close. He could not take criticism. On this point he was pathologically thin skinned, and he developed the belief that literary criticism only killed poetry, an attitude he was to maintain for most of his life. In a fit of grim humor he once called literary critics "wet dogs who force their way into our rooms and lie down in the best places." [34] But his resentment was deadly serious.

His increasing depression [35] during the years 1832–1833 had not only external but to a great degree also internal causes. He had reached a critical point in his development. He had exhausted his inspirational resources. New experiences, wider horizons, were necessary if he were to avoid being bogged down spiritually. He had to escape from the restricting conditions of Denmark and go out into the big, wide world.

He had planned for some time a trip abroad but had lacked the financial means. Fortunately, in Denmark the absolute monarchy displayed great understanding of the need for gifted talent to have the opportunity for spiritual renewal abroad. Each year the Royal Foundation *ad usus publicos* allocated grants to artists and scientists,[36] and in 1833 Hans Christian Andersen was among the applicants. Everybody was certain he would receive a grant; he himself was the only doubter, just as in his depression he totally doubted everything, himself, his abilities, and his possibilities of ever achieving his high artistic goal. Being the highly strung person that he was, he felt even physically ill.[37] But everything turned out right for, of course, he received the grant, his worries and sickness vanished, the world lay before him, he was rescued from stagnation. On 22 April 1833 he set forth.

IV   *The Great Journey*

A. Out into the Big, Wide World [38]

He was full of excitement and expectation about this great new adventure, and felt freer and happier than he had done for a long time. At first it was not easy to get used to the feeling of being free of cares. Even when he reached Hamburg he wrote to Edvard Collin saying that he no longer had his youthful zest for life. Just two years earlier he would have found happiness in traveling but "now the effect is different, though sufficient to save me from perishing." That, at least, was something, and very soon there was something else quite different to think about. Traveling in those days was a slow and tiresome business. To travel comfortably was only for those who were wealthy enough to own their own carriage: less fortunate souls were packed into cramped coaches, shaken, bumped, and covered with dirt on their slow journey along poor highways. Andersen amusingly described just how exhausting it all was in his "Goloshes of Fortune." The slowness had, however, a useful effect in that all one's worries from back home slowly dissolved before reaching a destination; the discomforts of traveling made the traveler forget all his usual preoccupations and prepared him for receiving new impressions.

Andersen clung passionately to all these new impressions, accepted the inconveniences with good humor, and forgot that he had lost his "youthful zest for life." He traveled by coach through Germany day and night, stopping a few times in the odd town. In Hamburg he visited a now long-forgotten Danish poet, Lars Kruse, who wrote the following prophetic prescription in Andersen's album when he was leaving,

> Stay what you are—faithful to nature and truth.
> Keep your soul pure and your heart full of youth.

Be Danish where Danish is spoken no more,
And European when returning to Denmark's shore.[39]

On 10 May he arrived in Paris, a city that made a great impression on him—with its parks, palaces, theaters, and its variety of life. In comparison Copenhagen appeared most provincial. Andersen stayed three months, saw all the sights, went to the theater, and started on a long dramatic poem based on a Danish ballad and called *Agnete and the Merman*.[40]

B. Italy at Last

Italy! This was the promised land for Danish artists and writers and had been so even back in the eighteenth century. Here one stood face to face with antiquity, here one could study and enjoy the master-pieces of the Renaissance, here were teeming, colorful crowds, magnificent scenery, and a climate that for the wind-blown and frost-bound Scandinavian was like a beautiful dream. Italy was an utter revelation for Andersen. He came via the Simplon Pass (the road that Napoleon, his father's great hero, had built) and first set foot on the holy soil of Italy on 18 September 1833. "A journey in Germany and France is really not foreign; the new world first comes on the other side of the Alps!" were his words back to Denmark.[42] He breathed deeply: the heavens were twice as high as those at home, the wind was a gentle fan, sweet chestnuts and figs grew by the wayside, clusters of grapes hung large and heavy, and the fishermen on Lake Maggiore sang with beautiful voices.[43] This was his idea of Paradise. Here he felt at home. He discovered that the warmth of the South was in his blood.

Nature and architecture made the first impressions: Milan's cathedral, the palaces of Genoa—he was overwhelmed. "If France is the country of reason, Germany and Denmark that of the heart, then Italy is the realm of the imagination. Everything is a painting!"[44]

From Genoa he went on to Pisa and Florence. Florence! He did not know where to stop or where to start when telling about all the splendors of the capital of Tuscany in his letters. The art of antiquity and the Renaissance swept him off his feet. It was only now that he began to realize what sculpture and painting were about and that Heiberg was right when he stressed the importance of a well-wrought artistic form. He felt that he was incompetent, ignorant, "life is so short, how do I find the time to learn so much!"[45]

He spent five quite bewildered days in Florence and on 13 October went on toward Rome, but was now finding out that all was not Paradise in Italy. On his journey from Milan to Genoa he had had to undergo "all the plagues and outrages to which Italy subjects a traveler," he wrote home.[46] From Florence to Rome things grew even worse, "Six days of misery brought us to the brink of despair. The beauty of Italy scarcely balances its dirtyness. It is a genuine pig-sty." The food was impossible to digest. When they eventually caught sight of Rome with the dome of St. Peter's floating above the city they were so exhausted, confessed Andersen, that their only thought was, "Now we can get something to eat!" [47]

C. The Eternal City

The Rome that Andersen and his two Danish traveling companions arrived in was in some respects little different from the one that today's tourist sees: the same streets and piazzas, the same fountains and monuments, the same churches, the same palaces, and to some degree the same collections of art. The city, though, was far smaller; there was no more than what lay within Aurelian's city walls: immediately outside them was the deserted Campagna. Certain buildings that dominate now did not exist then, such as the Vittorio Emanuele monument on the Capitol, nor did the wide boulevard down to the Colosseum, and the Forum was a large open field where cattle grazed on the soil that still covered the remnants of antiquity's buildings. Of course, everyday street life was quite different: the primitive peasant's carts, the laden donkeys, the ragged beggars, the pictures of the Madonna on the street corners, the Southern temperament that made people sing and dance in the evenings after the day's work, the atmosphere of gaiety, the colors and the piety on the great holy days—all this Hans Christian Andersen so supremely captured in his novel *The Improvisator*. In the daytime gaiety and noise ruled, while at night silence and not unrarely the deeds of darkness, murder, and assault in the poorly lit streets took place almost as frequently in reality as they did in novels.

The foreigners who visited Rome in those days were, first, a few relatively wealthy tourists attracted by the sun and the colorful life, and then the artists and scholars who went there to study. Numerous Danes holding grants from the Danish state visited Rome, and several Danish artists had been residents there for years. The Scandinavians kept together while the occasional German was admitted to their group; their uncrowned king was the Danish sculptor Bertel Thorvaldsen (1768–1844), who at that time was famous throughout Europe for such works as his Swiss lion in Lucerne, and who had been resident in Rome since 1797. Andersen was immediately admitted into this circle of colleagues and friends. He was actually not particularly well prepared for his visit to Rome, but made up for lost time with great energy and enthusiasm and, together with his countrymen, visited all the famous sights of the city and went on long excursions into the surrounding countryside.

His hectic sight-seeing was gradually replaced by a more detailed study of the masterpieces of Rome. During his four-month stay he paid twenty-five visits to museums and visited innumerable churches. He examined the works of art, discussed them with fellow-Danes, exercised his eye, formed his taste, and with each month became more independent in his judgment.

Naturally, he was constantly together with his countrymen, a companionship that gradually became somewhat tiresome. Among the things that bothered him was the fact that the Scandinavians practically turned their backs on Italy and the Italians. As good, enlightened Lutherans they indulgently shrugged their shoulders at the ordinary Italian's naiveté and his Catholic faith. Andersen had more sense; for he realized that this foreign religion had its own seriousness and was worthy of respect. He was far more open-minded than the majority of his fellow Danes.

D. Sorrows and Disappointments

His attitude was later to bear literary fruit, but meanwhile he had received two letters from Denmark that practically shattered his world. The first letter was from his fatherly guide Jonas Collin.[48] This arrived on the 16 December with the message that Hans Christian Andersen's mother had died at the old people's home in Odense. He had not seen much of her in later years, but her death affected him deeply. "Now I am completely alone," he wrote to a female acquaintance in Copenhagen, "no person is tied, by nature, to love me."[49] A bitter yet inescapable truth. This feeling of loneliness accompanied him for the rest of his life.

Jonas Collin's letter also contained bad news from another direction. Collin had asked Heiberg to pronounce judgment on a singspiel that Andersen had submitted to the Royal Theatre before his departure, and now here was the verdict. This experienced critic was of the opinion that Andersen was a lyrical improviser [50] and for that very reason lacked the balance and coolness essential for a dramatist; the conclusion was that this singspiel, at least, could not be recommended for performance. But there was worse to come. Andersen had sent back to Denmark the manuscript of that dramatic poem he had started in Paris. Unfortunately, this was a very indifferent work, showing Andersen to be still a romantic who believed that a work would be good if the poet was enthusiastic enough about his subject. Now Jonas Collin had to inform Andersen that everybody regarded the dramatic poem as a failure and that no publisher could be found for it.[51] This was a severe blow. But early in the next year (1834) he received a letter from his friend Edvard Collin,[52] who, apart from other disheartening news, most bluntly indicated the same view as Jonas Collin. The sensitive writer was profoundly shaken that his closest friend could be so brutally frank! [53] It took him a long time to recover from the disappointment he felt, and he did not resume correspondence with Edvard for many weeks.

Fortunately, Andersen was beginning to have other things to consider. His diary entry for 27 December 1833 has the following significant words, "this evening commenced on my novel *Improvisatoren* [*The Improvisator*]." This indicates that his urge to write was returning and that Heiberg's irritating (yet accurate) characterization of him had not only given him the title but also the idea for a novel about himself, only in Roman clothing.

He was soon well under way. Certainly the shock from Edvard's letter stunted his desire to write for a while, but in the long term it probably had an inspiring effect. He relived with greater intensity his own position in the world both as a writer and as a person: *ira facit versus*. Indignation and disappointment stimulated him.

In February the gay carnival festivities began (and he depicts them in *The Improvisator*). This old Roman festival with all forms of masquerades and horse racing down Il Corso was, for Andersen, an experience that helped remove his sorrows. When the merrymaking was over Andersen and two other Danes traveled to Naples, a journey that made him forget practically everything else.

E. See Naples and Die

Snow was falling on the Alban hills when the party crossed over, but on the coast it was summer. Almond trees were in bloom, oranges were being harvested, palm trees on the beach swayed in the wind while the blue, the indescribably blue, Mediterranean constantly tumbled upon the rocks. The further they drove south the more beautiful everything became. The scenery around Naples surpassed all that Andersen had ever seen: such colors, such luxuriance! great woods of vines, aloes the height of a man, air like a blissful kiss! "Only now do I know what Italy is! Yes, see Naples and die!" he exclaimed.[54] His enthusiasm knew no bounds.

But this was just the beginning. Fortune had it that Vesuvius was in eruption: lava was pouring down the mountain side, smoke came billowing up from the crater, and flames were reflected from above! What a backdrop for the human stage! There the men looked like demigods, the women like Madonnas, the children like Raphael-esque angels. Under his window, of an evening, the people sang serenades and played guitars, while he sat drinking Lacrymae Christi, the Vesuvian wine; and reflected on the house walls was the glow of the fiery lava streams. It was all too wonderful. "Here is my fatherland, for here I feel at home," he wrote.[55]

Fresh experiences flooded in; he heard the great contralto Malibran in Bellini's opera *Norma*, he was introduced to Neapolitan families, ascended the fire-spitting Vesuvius, went on excursions to Pompeii, Paestum—temples in the midst of wild, luxuriant nature—and further afield to Amalfi and Capri, where he was rowed into the Blue Grotto which had been discovered a few years earlier; "it was a fairyland that no poet could describe, no painter reproduce in colors. We floated in the blue ether while outside the waves were breaking against the steep rocks, where the red sea-apples grew like bloody tears," he said in a letter.[56]

It was with an indescribably heavy heart that he took leave of that south Italian paradise on 20 March. "Northward, northward lies the iron ring to fasten around my foot, there where my dear ones live in snow and fog. Yes, Denmark is a poor country! Italy received a horn overflowing with fruit and flowers while we only got a turf and a sloe hedge!"—was how he expressed his feelings about leaving.[57]

F. Back to the Cold North

On Palm Sunday 23 March he was back in Rome where he could recognize everything—it was like returning to Odense. He planned to stay for a week and to make full use of his time. He eagerly walked through the whole city revisiting his favorite places. During Easter he attended all the festivals in St. Peter's and numerous other churches as well as those in the streets and alleys. On his last evening he watched a magnificent fireworks display on the Tiber and went to a farewell party given by the Scandinavian colony; then it was time to leave. At dawn on 1 April he left the Eternal City.

The day itself was nasty, with horrible weather that grew worse; stormy and winter-cold up through Tuscany while his fellow travelers were deadly dull. The next day was his birthday, which he came to think of as he was drinking a ghastly cup of coffee between 4:00 and 5:00 in the morning in some wretched hostelry. He could only congratulate himself, and crawl back up into the coach to be rattled along on his way. Eventually, on 5 April, he reached Florence where he stayed for more than a week and felt quite at home. Via Bologna he came to Venice which seemed too dead to please him, though Titian's paintings interested him and he admired St. Mark's Square in the evening light. The lagoons with the fisherwomen waiting on the shore for their menfolk to return from the dangers of the sea drew his attention. North of the Apennines the scenery held little splendor for him after Rome and Naples so he shortened his route: Vicenza, Verona, Brenner, and then, farewell to Italy. The Alps closed behind him.

He stayed in Munich for several weeks and just as long in Vienna, where he made friends with interesting people and received many invitations. He went, of course, regularly to the Burg Theater where, being a well-known poet, he had a seat in the stalls at his disposal for the duration of his stay. In Dresden and Berlin the Vienna story repeated itself: many interesting people, many invitations, and much recognition. In Berlin Chamisso presented his friend Andersen with a volume of collected poems including his translations of five of Andersen's poems.[59] The newspapers mentioned his presence in the town—his fame was spreading. But, just as in Vienna, these pleasant experiences did not give him the pleasure that could have been expected. They were, so to speak, sandwiched between his two dominating emotional complexes: his radiant experiences in Italy and his anxiety concerning his homecoming.

The distaste at the thought of Denmark remained with him all the way from Naples.[60] Not one of his letters to Denmark fails to include some reference, often for no apparent reason, to the sorrows and insults heaped upon him in Denmark or that were going to be when he returned.[61] Although he was worried it is to be suspected that sometimes he was not unwilling to play the part of the persecuted and maltreated artist. Throughout his life he showed an inclination toward depressed and offended moods and often nurtured rather than tried to quell them, as many another person would have done in his place.

Besides this, on his homeward journey he fell victim to strongly conflicting emotions: [62] confidence in the feeling of having matured spiritually and at the same time a failing of confidence in his abilities; gratitude toward God and distaste for the pettiness of affairs at home. To write poetry was beyond him, or so he claimed. To a friend in Copenhagen he wrote, "Oh, if only I could find the power to produce the picture that lives in my soul; I would then have done something worthwhile. But I cannot, and I lack both the desire and courage to try" [63]—which sounds strange considering that in Munich, where he wrote this letter, he had been hard at work on his *The Improvisator* and had already been working on it in Rome and, to some degree, in Naples.

The truth of the matter was probably that he was in that confused state of mind that often, in a creative artist, is a sign that something new is on the way, a new work is about to be born; a condition where hope and doubt coexist. Birth or miscarriage? Can or cannot? But the crucial conflict in Andersen's case was undoubtedly between the pleasure he found in Italy and the despair he felt over what he considered his troubles in Denmark. Out of this conflict grew his novel *The Improvisator*.

In fact, his reception in Copenhagen was touching and sincere, for, naturally, his friends and particularly the Collin family were fond of him and had missed him. In the streets people called to him saying, "Welcome home!" In those days Copenhagen was a small town and everybody knew the strange-looking writer. He stayed with friends for a while and then on 1 September rented some rooms by the harbor at 18 Nyhavn.

V *World Fame*

A. The New Hans Christian Andersen [64]

Andersen was now thirty. Was he himself aware of the great changes that had taken place in him? He probably had an inkling. His friends noticed that he seemed far more independent, and no wonder. His spiritual world had been greatly enlarged. In his thoughts he lived not only in Denmark but also in Europe. He had seen and experienced new people and fresh scenery; he had discovered painting and sculpture. His expansive temperament had found room to move in: that he had delayed his return as much as possible was not just because insults and other affronts were awaiting, but also because Denmark was too limiting for him. Moreover, in Italy he had discovered himself, and understood that his spirit was more of the South than of the cold North, a cosmopolitan just as much as a Dane. Finally, his year-long journey had put Denmark at a suitable and necessary distance and enabled him to look upon his fatherland with fresh eyes, and on home affairs with at least a greater sense of superiority than before. Moreover, as a writer he had had time to settle down and replace his romantic ideals and poetic habits with new ones that were his own.

To begin with, he had to complete his Italian novel that was well under way, and he did so rapidly. By November the manuscript was ready for the printer. But the book was not published until April 1835. In the meantime Andersen was in urgent need of money. His occasional poems and other minor writings yielded an insufficient income, and as the winter wore on his situation became increasingly difficult. In May he had to turn to "Father Collin" for help. A strange ironical twist of fate, for *The Improvisator* was published in Danish on 9 April and the first slender volume of fairy tales on 8 May, the two works which were to be the foundation of his world-wide reputation. Nevertheless, there he was in Copenhagen without knowing how to obtain money for the rent, for clothes, or for repairing the holes in his boots.

His finances remained uncertain for several years. He scraped through as best he could, making do with the small sums that his books and plays brought in. It was not until 1838 that his income stabilized, for then, after petitioning to the king, he received a modest annual grant.

Meanwhile he was engaged in feverish activity: a number of singspiele (which are of no interest today), the first thirteen fairy tales, and no less than three novels. The first was *The Improvisator* (1835), then *O.T.* (1836), and, finally, *Only a Fiddler* (1837).

In Denmark his first two novels were favorably received by both the reading public and the critics, while the third met with indifference, at least, from the critics—the exception being the young philosopher Søren Kierkegaard (1813–1855),[65] whose devastating criticism will be discussed below. His hard judgment together with the fact that the Royal Theatre had rejected his somewhat insipid plays gave the doubting Andersen the impression that people did not want to recognize him as a writer in his own country. This impression was strengthened by the enormous success that his novels were enjoying in Germany. *Only a Fiddler* in particular was widely read and greatly admired. He was determined, however, to turn the criticism and make a name for himself as a dramatist in Denmark, and he actually did succeed. The play was a five-act, rhymed drama in the style of romanticism called *The Mulatto* and was first performed in 1840. Andersen felt proud and happy after this success and decided to follow it with another play of the same sort entitled *The Moorish Girl*. By working intensely the play was completed in the summer of 1840, but it only brought him trouble and disappointment. The Royal Theatre eventually accepted it after reservations and the performance was constantly postponed. The author, who was obsessed with a pathological impatience, was beginning to suspect animosity and petty spite from all quarters. In his bitterness he decided to leave everything behind him and go abroad.

B.   To Greece and the Balkans

His journey took him first to Germany and Italy but initially gave him little pleasure. His beloved Rome was a great disappointment, but then the same experience the second time around can rarely compare with the first. In addition, the winter of 1840–1841 was noted for its particularly poor weather. Andersen felt ill, and a letter from Denmark informed him that his latest play had failed.[66] It is easy to imagine his state of mind. He did not recover from his depression until, unexpectedly, he received an extra grant from the king of Denmark enabling him to extend his journey to Greece and Constantinople. From Naples he sailed via Malta to Athens where he spent a month before continuing to Constantinople—a unique experience, since very few Danes had traveled so far, and if anyone knew how to value the new and picturesque that person was Andersen. Yet that was not enough, for he decided, despite many warnings, to return home by sailing up the Danube to Vienna, a journey that no Dane had yet accomplished. Parts of the Ottoman Empire were in revolt, and Andersen was full of grave misgivings, but when it counted this nervous man's curiosity was always greater than his weaknesses. "My desire to see new things is so great," he wrote, "that it overcomes my fears. I take the boat. After all, God lives." [67] He chanced the journey

and arrived safe and sound in Vienna. In the summer of 1841 he was
back in Copenhagen.

For the second time in his life a long journey abroad saved him
from the disappointments of Copenhagen and restored him to harmony with himself and the world. Sick and depressed he had turned
his back on Copenhagen; revived and healthy he had returned.
Andersen had experienced so much on his journey that he was able to
write a book about it which appeared in 1842 with the title *En Digters
Bazar* (*A Poet's Bazaar*). Written with animation and sparkling spirits
this was his best travel book; it is a bright contrast to the gloomy
circumstances that precipitated his journey.

C.   The Pinnacle of Success [68]

His long journey signaled the start of a highly significant period in
Andersen's eventful life, one in which he was bestowed with the
richest of gifts, for better or worse. This was to be his period of
greatest triumphs, bitterest disappointments, of events of great national importance, and of the maturity of his artistic abilities. The
1840s saw Andersen at his peak. Within this period his dreams of
world-wide fame were realized to such a degree that he really did
have to pinch himself and ask whether it was he, the pauper child,
who had come so far.

On his very first visit to Germany in 1831 he gained many friends
among the leading artists and writers, and in subsequent years had
won more. The German reading public had come to hear about his
unusual life via such channels as a widely read 1838 encyclopedia
article about him. By the end of the 1830s, his three novels and the
first fairy tales had been printed in German. The German translation
of *A Poet's Bazaar* came out in 1843. On his second long journey he
had seen for himself that his works were known as far as Athens and
Constantinople, and at Leipzig no end of compliments were paid
him.[69]

Yet this acclaim scarcely compared with that which he was soon to
receive. In Paris in 1843 the leading French writers of the day
(Balzac, Hugo, Lamartine, and Dumas, as well as Heine and the
famous actress Rachel) received him as their equal, and the following
year in Germany praise flowed in from all sides. His books were on
display in bookshops wherever he went, and fellow travelers on
coach, ship, or train expressed their admiration for his works. One
lady admirer in Brunswick went so far as to cry, "Ich liebe Sie! Ja, ich

liebe Sie!" And, continued Andersen in a letter, "she was quite pretty, but married! I did not know what to say, so I kissed her hand and then shook hands with her husband so that he would not feel left out." [70]

Poets and men of letters flocked around him everywhere he went, and he made friends with the leading musicians of the period: Mendelssohn, Schumann, and Liszt. A great highlight came with his presentation at the court of Weimar where the young hereditary grand duke struck up a warm friendship with him—a friendship that was to last for many years. [71] From now on, all doors were to be open to him.

He had only two disappointments in Germany; he was to have been presented to the king of Prussia, but the latter had just left Berlin; the second disappointment was more humiliating. In Berlin he called on old Jacob Grimm, the famous collector of fairy tales, but Grimm had never even heard of his name, and had to ask Andersen what he had written! This incident was more amusing to Andersen's German friends than to himself, and they had to console him by telling him that Grimm was always thirty years behind his time. [72] It was also in 1844 that he received pleasing recognition in Denmark: he was invited to be the guest of King Christian VIII on the North Frisian island of Föhr (then part of the kingdom of Denmark), where the royal family were spending the summer. It was in September, and exactly twenty-five years had passed since his first arrival in Copenhagen. "How curious is Providence," he wrote to Edvard Collin, "my heart is strangely warmed for it is now twenty-five years ago since I came to Copenhagen with my little bundle, a poor, unknown boy." [73] Now he sat at the king's table. He was full of gratitude, and probably pride as well; there was reason for both.

The following year, when he was again traveling south, he was received at all the courts and he read his tales aloud in German to much enthusiasm and admiration. Mendelssohn broke out, "But you read superbly, no one reads fairy tales like you do!" [74] In Berlin large publishing houses fought for the right to publish a de luxe edition of his collected works. The printing rights went to a Leipzig publisher, the Danish born Carl Lorck. For this German edition Andersen wrote the first of his autobiographies, *Das Märchen meines Lebens ohne Dichtung* (1847); an English edition with the title *The True Story of My Life* was published in the same year.

D. A Visit to Britain [75]

Andersen was soon immersed in writing a new novel, *The Two Baronesses*, and in learning English. In England interest had been growing in his work; his first three novels had already been translated in 1845 and translations of his fairy tales soon followed. It was time, he thought, to put in an appearance, for, as in Germany, his presence would stimulate interest in him both as a person and as a writer.

In June 1847 he traveled to England via Holland, where his books had long been known and where he was celebrated by all leading Dutch men of letters. He was deeply gratified but not surprised, for he was growing accustomed to being regarded as a European figure. Nevertheless, when he arrived in London at the end of June his reception almost took his breath away. During his six weeks in London he was feted and celebrated to exhaustion. He was pleased with his fame but admitted that it had its price. Meeting so many people was tremendously exhausting for him, and having to speak English with them was a trial for both him and them; his English was so bad that Dickens had had to ask him to speak Danish as that language was easier for him to understand. He made a visit to Scotland too, but the innumerable invitations tired him out completely, so that he was compelled to leave. By September he was back in Copenhagen.

One of the objectives of his journey to England had been to negotiate the continued publication of his books and to meet fellow writers. As soon as he arrived he contacted the London publisher Richard Bentley, who had published his first three novels, and Mary Howitt, who had been responsible for their translation. Bentley was to become a loyal friend and a faithful collaborator, who made every possible effort to make Andersen's works available to the English reading public but who, reluctantly, had eventually to bring publication to a standstill when the market became flooded with pirated editions. The good relations with Mary Howitt, on the other hand, soon disintegrated. She translated mainly from German, but also knew Swedish, and, in time, some Danish. She was a very enterprising woman who seemed to want a complete monopoly of Andersen in England. Here Andersen was of another opinion, and, in anger, she broke off relations with him and later spoke very slightingly of him, even in print.

The hectic social life into which Andersen had been thrown from the very start of his visit to England brought him into contact with many people from the literary world, among them the elderly editor and critic W. Jerdan, who in two reviews in 1845 was the first to draw the attention of the English-reading public to the Danish writer, and who later never lost an opportunity to praise both the man and his writings.

But Andersen's greatest experience was his friendship with Dickens—a friendship that was to have a strange course. It began with mutual literary admiration. The two writers had read each other's books (a number of Dickens's early novels appeared in Danish in the 1840s) and thus they, in a way, knew each other when they first met at a London dinner party. The meeting was touching. "We took each other by both hands, gazed in each other's eyes, talked and understood each other, and on the veranda [where they continued their conversation] tears came into my eyes," was Andersen's entry in his diary (16 July 1847). A few weeks later on his return from Scotland, Andersen visited the Dickens family at their summer residence near Ramsgate, the port from which Andersen's boat to the Continent was to sail. The reunion was convivial and rewarding for both parties. Andersen returned to his hotel in Ramsgate that evening, but the following morning when the boat was to leave Dickens stood on the quay to say good-bye once more, a gesture that touched Andersen deeply.

The exchange of letters between them during the following years was cordial but came to a halt in 1851, only to be resumed in 1856 when Dickens, on receiving a letter from Andersen, wrote to invite him to stay a week or two with him as his guest. Whether Dickens was sincere about the invitation is difficult to determine, but Andersen readily took him at his word and the visit took place in June the following year (1857). For a variety of reasons the visit lasted not a week or two, but actually five weeks, and this turned out to be too much. Dickens's family grew tired of having this strange and egocentric Dane living in their house for so long. That Dickens himself also became irritated was something that Andersen was never to realize and he was greatly saddened on departing from "my home with Dickens" (as Andersen expressed it in a letter to Copenhagen), and from Dickens himself, who had been "like a loving brother" to him. [76]

Andersen was not to know that the family, including Dickens himself, breathed a sigh of relief on his departure, nor that his visit had taken place at an extremely inconvenient time: Dickens was even busier than usual, and moreover was at the point of breaking up his marriage (he separated from his wife soon afterward), and on top of all this, Dickens's enthusiasm for the friendship was, eventually, much less than Andersen's. This last point is clearly illustrated by the condescending tone that Dickens used in letters to his friends at that period when describing his fellow writer from Denmark. In truth, the two men were far too different in temperament for any lasting friendship to develop. Nor can it be denied that Andersen, with all his worries and self-centeredness (and his poor English), must have been extremely trying to have at close quarters for any length of time. Moreover, there is evidence that Mary Howitt, who knew Dickens well, had played her part in cooling Dickens's sympathy for Andersen.

Soon after his departure Andersen wrote a long and touching letter expressing his gratitude, to which Dickens eventually replied in a somewhat cool and conventional tone, but he never wrote to Andersen again. In subsequent years Andersen wrote numerous letters to him but to his consternation and sorrow he never received a reply. Clearly Dickens wished to break off their relationship. Nevertheless, Andersen for his part maintained his warm feelings for his silent friend, and Dickens's death in 1870 moved him deeply.

E. In Love for the Last Time

During these golden years Andersen suffered a grievous disappointment. He experienced what was to be the last great passion of his life, one that was as unhappy as that for Riborg Voigt, his first love. His affection was focused on Jenny Lind, the Swedish singer. This eminent artist was a natural stage performer, and Mendelssohn had said that a personality such as hers had not been born in centuries.[77] In 1838, at the age of eighteen, she had created a furore with her debut in Stockholm as Agathe in Weber's *Der Freischütz* while her European career had started in 1843 at the Royal Theatre in Copenhagen, which was where Andersen met her.[78]

Her portraits do not allow any conclusion to be drawn about her appearance, for they are so very different, presumably because hers was that animated, dynamic temperament that has so many faces. There was no doubt, however, about her immediate charm, that powerful radiation which only rarely can be portrayed in a picture and which captivates all who encounter it. Andersen was no exception, and he fell in love almost at once. He was regularly in attendance, either at parties thrown by Danish friends or alone with her, and she could hardly have been in any doubt about his feelings for her. When she was about to leave Copenhagen Andersen handed her a letter "which she must understand," as his entry in his almanac (20 September 1843) has it.[79] Yet she kept him at a distance, probably because she did not wish to marry at the beginning of her career—at any rate not Andersen. "Friendship, but nothing more!" is the mint's response to the butterfly's proposal in the fairy tale "The Butterfly": a reply very apposite to Andersen's own situation in 1843.

Two years later, in October 1845, when Jenny Lind was again in Copenhagen, Andersen began to realize that his chances were dwindling. At a farewell party she gave for her Danish friends at her hotel, she expressed her thanks to Bournonville, the ballet master, for taking such good care of her and for being a father to her in Copenhagen. In his response Bournonville declared that now all the men in Denmark would want to be his children so that they might be Jenny Lind's brothers. "That would be far too many," she said, "I would prefer to choose one of them to be my brother for all the others. Will you be that brother, Andersen?" and with a champagne glass in her hand she went over and touched glasses with him. There could be no mistake, and the wretched writer had to make the best of it and drink a toast to brotherhood.[80] Forget her, he could not; there was hope that her feelings might change. At any rate, on his journey southward that year he took care to arrive in Berlin in December when she too would be there. He had hoped they would celebrate Christmas together and so he turned down all invitations. He sat waiting in his hotel room but she did not send word. At eight o'clock he gave up and went out to some German friends. The next day, when, not without bitterness, he told her how he had spent Christmas Eve, she laughed and said, "It did not occur to me for I thought you were with princes and princesses. Moreover, I had been invited out. But now we will have Christmas Eve again, and I will have the candles lit for the child! On New Year's Eve there will be a tree here with me!"[81] So it came to pass, and this romantic meeting of the two Scandinavian children was the subject of many rumors and was mentioned in the papers. Andersen himself described the occasion in his German autobiography in 1847. Their friendship was thus becoming a matter for all Europe and, to some degree, helped enhance the publicity surrounding his visit to England the following year, particularly since, scarcely by chance, his visit happened to coincide with Jenny Lind's appearances there in opera. However, they were both heavily engaged in their activities and only met a few times in London. Hereafter she disappeared from his life. In 1850 she started on her American tour and two years later married a German pianist in Boston. Andersen met the happy couple in Vienna in 1854, but by that time his former love for her had subsided. This was their last meeting.

F. National events

The political upheavals of 1848 occupied much of his thoughts and feelings. For centuries friendly relations had existed between Denmark and the German states, and the cultural links had always been strong and fruitful. In the sixteenth century it was Luther and not Calvin who brought the Reformation to Denmark, and throughout the subsequent centuries large numbers of Danish theologians studied at German universities. Danish authors were received in Germany as kindred spirits, as Andersen himself had experienced when visiting Denmark's giant neighbor in the 1830s.

From the fifteenth century the duchies of Holstein and Slesvig had been closely linked to Denmark though with partial independence. German was spoken in Holstein and parts of Slesvig without influencing the relationship with Denmark. The Holsteiners were loyal Danish subjects and during the eighteenth century and the beginning of the nineteenth numbers of them attained high posts in the administration of the Danish monarchy. However, the nationalistic ideas of romanticism changed this situation. The concept that language indicated national affiliation brought the Holsteiners and numbers of Slesvigians to the conclusion that they ought to be associated with Germany. This conclusion, linked with the liberal ideas sweeping Europe, led in the 1830s and 1840s to increasing opposition to Danish absolutism. An active group of German nationalists in the two duchies openly agitated for closer ties with the German confederation. The situation grew tense, and in 1848 a rising broke out which received military support from Prussia. The war lasted for nearly three years until the political state of affairs in Europe caused Prussia to withdraw support. The rising was put down in 1850 and the two duchies remained associated with Denmark.

Andersen was deeply affected by these national events [82] and put the patriotic feelings of the moment into a number of poems. The sufferings of the nation were also his, as were the rejoicings after victory. He, too, mourned the loss of friends who had died in the fighting.

In order to set his painful involvement at a distance, in 1849

Andersen went on a three-month journey through Sweden, [83] a country which, strangely enough, was little visited in those days by the Danes. Once again his reputation almost swamped him. His writings were known everywhere and once more he was feted and celebrated—so much so that in a letter he confessed that he never had peace for one moment because of the attention shown him.[84] The host of impressions of land and waterscapes, and of people, provided the material for another travel book which was published as *In Sweden* in 1851.

That Andersen was able to find the time to write as much as he did during this eventful decade is quite remarkable, for he was continually traveling, both abroad and in Denmark and, moreover, was deeply absorbed in national events. His productivity seems to have been at its best when things were happening either to him or about him. Throughout his life he gave thanks to Providence for the joy of being able to write creatively, but during the 1840s he had more reason to do so than ever before. His writings from this period display powers of concentration, intensity of feeling, and mastery of form that indicate a peaking of his genius. In 1842 his most substantial and liveliest travel book, *A Poet's Bazaar*, appeared; one of his best novels, *The Two Baronesses*, was published in 1848, while in 1851 came his travel book *In Sweden*. Nevertheless, during these restless, happy years, in between the major undertakings, he was able to find both time and energy to write a number of his most inspired fairy tales: "The Nightingale," "The Ugly Duckling," "The Snow Queen," "The Bell," "The Shadow," "The Story of a Mother," and many more. He was even able to keep up his writing for the stage. These accomplishments are evidence of a remarkable display of energy, the more so considering his sensitive constitution and recurring attacks of nervous exhaustion and other weaknesses both physical and mental. That indomitable will of his to live coupled with his enormous need to create saw him through.

VI *Later Years*

A. The Famous Bohemian [85]

When the war ended and his latest travel book was completed, Andersen was a tired man; as usual, depression accompanied his exhaustion. His creative activities, his sorrows and joys were telling on him. In the summer of 1850 the reaction was setting in, and he wrote despondently to a friend, "The feeling of not having achieved anything worthwhile, and the conviction that I cannot do so, often tortures me greatly." [86] Likewise, he wrote to Edvard Collin, at about the same time, complaining, "I no longer have the carefree mind and hopes of youth; they were with me long. There is no ambition for me to strive for with all my heart, there is nothing within reason to achieve! . . . my life seems to be in the past, and that is my ·sorrow." [87]

His depression was an indication that he was at a turning point. Fortunately, as a writer he was far from finished. More than half of his total output of fairy tales, or stories as he now preferred to call them, were written in the last decades of his life, the best of them coming well up to his earlier standards. In the 1850s he interrupted his tales while working on a new version of his memoirs based on *Das Märchen meines Lebens*. This new autobiography appeared in Danish in 1855 with the title *Mit Livs Eventyr*. After he had completed another novel, *To Be, or Not To Be?* (1857), he returned to writing fairy tales and continued to do so until a few years prior to his death. Andersen also managed within these final years to write a short but masterly sixth novel, *Lucky Peer* (1870), as well as two plays and numerous poems, many for specific private and public occasions.

The fears that Andersen expressed in his letter to Edvard Collin were of another nature; when a person with such a restless, ambitious temperament as Andersens' fulfills his high aims a crucial moment is reached. Stagnation can set in, replacing struggle and action. Andersen's high ambitions had now been realized. His writings had conquered the world, and society had no higher peak to climb. Even if the subsequent years brought fresh events and impressions, unavoidably much seemed to be mere repetition. Andersen had to reconcile himself to the fact that the major experiences of his were behind him.

Stability had also entered his material affairs. He was now financially independent, in an unassuming way, and he could order his life as he pleased and travel wherever he wished. The awkward and insecure youngster from the provinces had, with the years, changed into an elegant and distinguished man of the world, correct yet cordial, an aristocrat who carried himself with such sureness and distinction that no one could guess that he had grown up in poverty. [88] He was an international figure, and he knew it. His very manner showed his awareness. He felt completely at home in his role as a famous and admired person. It is true that at times he could be somewhat difficult to get on with; yet when he felt at ease he radiated cordiality and delighted everyone with his sparkling wit. Despite his oddities he was a welcome guest everywhere.

He never married. By nature he was a bohemian, and his restlessness prevented him from settling down to a regular family life. When in Copenhagen he lived in rented rooms or stayed at a hotel. He never really liked Copenhagen,[89] but he could not be without the Royal Theatre, and his friends; his visits to them were a substitute for a home and family of his own. But he would never stop long in the city. He would often stay for periods as a guest at various Danish manor houses; each year he would go abroad, usually to Germany, Austria, and Switzerland, occasionally to Paris; he was twice in London, once in Spain, and even once in Portugal, a country that Danes rarely visited in those days. He was often invited to America but hesitated at the thought of the long crossing. His fears were reinforced in 1858 when one of his dearest friends was lost in the disaster that struck the German liner *Austria* when she caught fire and sank.[90]

His international fame was stable and assured. In Denmark the criticism that had vexed him for so long was now silent, and he was regarded as a national monument.[91] Even socially in Denmark he was at the top. Andersen was regularly invited to the Danish court and when, in later years, he was too weak to go out, King Christian IX (king, 1863–1906) came to visit him on several occasions.

One of his greatest triumphs came to him in his old age when, in December 1867, his native town of Odense awarded him the freedom of the town.[92] His reply to the city council's letter shows how deeply moved he was by this honor, and it also shows the modesty with which he regarded his life's successes. The festivities in Odense [93] were a tremendous experience to him; a grand official banquet at the city hall, a torchlight procession in his honor, and the whole town illuminated, just as the wise woman had prophesied when he was a boy. Naturally, the people of Odense had read *The Story of My Life* in which Andersen had described in detail the prophecy, and nothing could have been more reasonable than that the people of his native town would see to it that it came true.

Alas, poor Andersen was hardly able to enjoy all the homage paid him. He was emotionally overcome, he suffered from a chill, a raging toothache, and rheumatic pains, and he had to admit in a letter that he "was only a mortal, tied by the frailties of the flesh."

B. The Final Years

The last twenty-five years of his life were without epoch-making experiences. Of course, Denmark's second war with Prussia in 1864 made a terrible impression on him. Bismarck had a number of reasons for wishing to settle the problem of the two duchies, which were Danish though in part German speaking. His modern army easily defeated the out-numbered, poorly equipped Danish troops, and Denmark had to sign a peace treaty which forced her to surrender Holstein and Slesvig to Prussia. This was a national disaster, and Andersen, wedded as he was to his art, was absolutely bewildered by these harsh political and military realities. Personally the war meant to him that he would no longer visit his German friends. In his diary for 16 April 1864 he noted down the following lines of despair: "I feel every kindness that has been shown to me in Germany, acknowledge my friends there, and feel as a Dane that I must totally break with them all; they have been torn out of my heart, never again can we meet." He also broke off relations with Grand Duke Alexander of Weimar, who regrettably had taken an active part in the war on the German side, and they never met again. "I cannot and will not be among Germans," Andersen wrote in a letter.[94]

With time, other and more important changes in his private life were to take place. With no family or relatives of his own he gradually felt a real need for a home. When Jonas Collin died in 1861 at age eighty-five, the "home of homes" was closed and Andersen's loneliness made itself felt. Formerly his extensive writing and restless traveling had compensated for his loneliness, but now with age it was becoming a grievous burden. His state of health was also troublesome. He had never been robust though his tall, strongly built body might convey a different impression. Andersen appears to have been neurasthenic from birth, and this gave rise throughout his life to such symptoms as fainting, dizziness, depressions, and other nervous disorders. He was nearly always feeling ill. From 1860 on his energy began to fail and the nervous disorders worsened.[95] He was no longer able to make such great efforts as before and gradually became the helpless victim of his impressions, even the most trifling.

Thus it was becoming increasingly difficult for him to lead his bohemian life. Fortunately, in 1862 he had made friends with the wealthy Jewish family of the name Melchior in Copenhagen.[96] Here were people who understood his difficulties, and they readily opened their home to him. He was deeply grateful for their hospitality and came to need it more and more, particularly after 1868 when his strength began to fail him in earnest. Now it was more than a matter of nerves; recurrent feverish attacks, a weight on his chest, and fainting fits were indications of serious illness. Nevertheless, he was still able to travel abroad, though in 1873 he wrote back from Switzerland with melancholic self-irony: "I sometimes have a feeling in my midriff as if I had been broken into two and riveted together again but poorly." On his return journey by rail he fainted twice.[97] This was to be his last journey abroad. It is generally assumed that he suffered from cancer of the liver, though this diagnosis is uncertain as there were strong indications of rapidly progressive sclerosis.[98] However that may be, the end was plain, yet death came slowly. He lived to enjoy his seventieth birthday on 2 April 1875;[99] perhaps the expectation had kept him going, and he was not disappointed. The day proved an orgy of tributes from the whole world: flowers and telegrams, deputations from Odense and Copenhagen, a special audience with the king and queen, a gala performance at the Royal Theatre, and a dinner party at the Melchior's.

His best day had given him much pleasure but had also greatly exhausted him. Two months later he was so weak that the Melchiors moved him out to their house on the outskirts of Copenhagen. His condition was hopeless, and death occurred on 4 August.[100] Andersen had been happy, easy in his mind, and free of pain during his last days and had slipped peacefully and imperceptibly into unconsciousness.

The funeral service was held on 11 August,[101] and not one tenth of the mourners could fit inside Copenhagen's Cathedral. The obituaries in the Copenhagen press, as could be expected, contain only praise and respect for the man and his works. The *Berlingske Tidende* carried a detailed assessment of his achievements as a writer, and emphasized his rich and gentle humor, his imagination and keen eye for the small characteristic detail that found so natural expression in the fairy tales. "He never lapsed into dry allegory, for his fairy tales were not made from the abstract; he saw characteristics in concrete objects and gave them form according to his sovereign creative will." Within the brief tale he was a great psychologist. "His words, chosen with great precision, always hit the nail on the head." Another newspaper wrote that Andersen had known how "to strike chords that reverberated in every human breast."

VII *Personality*

A. Personal Documents

Andersen left more personal documents than most other artists:
two autobiographies (intended for the public), an enormous number
of letters (to friends), and a series of comprehensive diaries (intended
for himself). Through these documents it is possible to follow the
events of his life and at the same time to obtain a varied picture of his
strange personality.

His first large memoir was published in German in 1847. Eight
years later (1855), when the writer was fifty years old, he published
the revised and extended version in Danish, which, however,
attracted little attention abroad. Only a single translation was made
during Andersen's lifetime, an American one (1871), to which, at the
request of the publisher Andersen added a brief description of the
period 1855–1867. In Europe, though, it was *Das Märchen meines
Lebens ohne Dichtung* that was read. This book was a great international success because of the moving picture of his life: his poverty in
Odense, his difficult time as a young man, his struggle to make a name
for himself as a writer and the European successes that gradually
crowned his efforts—a drama concluding, naturally, with the confi-
dent affirmation that he had achieved his highest hopes.
Furthermore, the account is spiced with a host of picturesque and
moving details.

The main concern of the memoir is the difficulty that Andersen had
in overcoming the numerous obstacles in his way. He maintained that
he only became accepted in his own country as a great writer after he
had achieved such extensive world-wide fame that the Danes had to
capitulate. In short, while Denmark had tried to suppress him,
Europe had rescued him. In his own time, and even later, this view of
his life was widely accepted. The Danish critic Georg Brandes, in an
essay,[102] called him, "the hunted animal of Danish literature." In the
twentieth century, however, Danish scholars began to doubt the
correctness of this picture. Penetrating studies, above all by the late
H. Topsøe-Jensen, reveal that Andersen's account is one-sided and
on occasion distorted. It has become increasingly clear that Andersen
omitted many facts that did not really harmonize with his main
concern, and he unduly emphasized others. The picture is indeed a
highly subjective, emotional one. The sequence of events has more
than once been reversed in order to make a dramatic point. Of

course, his memoirs are not and could not be a sober account, a quiet reflection upon an eventful life; they had to be rather an explanation and a defense, a settling of accounts with real and imaginary antagonists. Andersen wanted to prove to the reading public that he had been ill-treated and misunderstood in Denmark, and his memoirs were to be that "proof."

This self-obsession, and his eagerness to be seen in a certain light, influence his book more than is good for it. But they show only one side of his personality. A far truer picture is obtained from his letters to his friends, nearly all of which have been published. As early as 1878 an excellent selection was put into book form by two of Andersen's journalist friends, Bille and Bøgh, and published as *Breve fra Hans Christian Andersen*. Many letters, too, were published by Andersen's friend Edvard Collin, in *H. C. Andersen og det Collinske Hus* (1882). In the twentieth century, letters to practically every one of his friends have been published in a long series of individual collections, nearly all of them under guidance of H. Topsøe-Jensen. In this connection may be mentioned *H. C. Andersens nærmeste Omgang* (1918), the memoirs of Rigmor Stampe, who was related to the Collins family and who knew Andersen well. In the letters the poet presents himself as he is, almost without reservations. Here he converses about a variety of things, and it is almost possible to sense his moods, as they fluctuate between gay humor and dark melancholy.

Finally, there are his diaries (published 1971–1976) which he kept almost all his life, and which represent the writer's *vie intime*. Here he committed to paper a good deal that he did not tell in his letters; here, among other things, he kept an extremely meticulous record of his physical and psychical condition day by day.

B. Psychic Constitution

The picture revealed to the reader through these three groups of documents is extraordinarily complicated. When looking back on his exceptional career Andersen felt that his life had been a happy one. [103] Still, his memoirs, letters, and above all, diaries, leave an almost appalling impression of how heavy life must have been for him.

In the first place, his health was extremely delicate, and his nervous constitution made him a prey to many harmful impressions. The thick-skinned protection that most people have against their experi-

ences was not his. Everything went directly into him and took posses-
sion of his whole personality at every moment. The turn of his moods
was sudden, violent, and complete. When he had written the fairy
tale "The Story of a Mother," he joyfully ran to read it aloud to
Henriette Collin (Edvard Collin's wife), without stopping to consider
that a few years earlier she herself had lost a child. As soon as he
realized his terrible thoughtlessness, he completely forgot his story,
fell at her feet, kissed her hands, and cried with her. The impact of
her sorrow had immediately obliterated his joy over the new story
which just a moment before had so completely occupied him.[104]
Strikingly, he himself wrote in a letter in 1855, "I am as water.
Everything moves me. Everything is reflected in me. I suppose it is
part of my writer's nature, and often have I had pleasure and blessing
from it, but it is often also a torment." [105]

To his sensibility must be added a number of peculiarities strongly
contrasting his great intellectual stature. Far beyond his boyhood he
gave the impression of being a big child. There was truth in this, for
he did retain for years certain characteristics normally found in
children: the immediate relation to things around him, the sudden
reversal of moods, the unreflecting pleasure, or sorrow, over matters
big and small without distinction, and, not least, pleasure in his own
achievements. Adults also feel these things but do not display them
except after much consideration.

There were other points where he appeared immature, for example, in his cautious relation to women. Without doubt, this restraint
had some external causes. Many people have found that dependence
or pressure experienced during youth has later prevented them from
relating to persons of the opposite sex. Such feelings of inferiority
were only too well-known to Andersen, and these were further
accentuated by his being conscious of his own unprepossessing
appearance and of being different from other people. However, while
most people get over such difficulties with time, Andersen did not.
When he was in love he could not bring himself to take the decisive
and essential initiative. The only occasion when he did actually make
a serious effort was over his love for Jenny Lind, and then he was
turned down. It is understandable that because of his bohemian
nature, his nervous irritability, and his feeling of the demands of an
artist's calling he had serious reservations about committing himself
to marriage. But neither did he dare to pluck the bloom of eroticism
from a casual love affair. The descriptions in *The Improvisator* of

Antonio's temptations and his reactions to them draw a very accurate picture of Andersen's own state of mind.

In addition to his so-called childishness, Andersen was distinquished by a high-reaching ambition that dated to his childhood: he had to rise in society, he had to become a famous writer, greater than all others. He often claimed that his thirst for fame was out of regard for his benefactors and his country; those at home must see that their efforts to help him onward had not been in vain, and that he brought honor to the name of Denmark in foreign countries. His intentions were sincere. Nevertheless, he did not deny that ambition was the primary stimulus to writing.[106]

However, his vanity was what people in little Copenhagen talked about most. From the start he had in his nature a desire to draw attention to himself, an inclination to always see himself from the outside, an irresistible urge to observe how he appeared to other people. What do they say about me? was the question he was always asking. It is also true, as he claimed in his younger years, that he had to write much in order to earn a living, but a great contributing factor was his headlong rush to be in the eyes of the public.

C. Psychic Conflicts

What was even stranger than his immaturity, his excessive ambition, and his often quite ridiculous self-centeredness is the fact that these peculiarities appeared side by side with contrary tendencies limiting and crossing them in highly complex interplay. Immature characteristics remained with him nearly all his life, while at the same time he had acquired an extraordinary knowledge of the world, a tactfulness and sense of occasion that only adults with a wealth of experience come to possess. Just how tactful he could be is revealed by an episode that took place in 1844 when he was the guest of King Christian VIII on the island of Föhr. One evening the king enquired about his financial situation and let it be understood that he would be of assistance at any time if Andersen were to need anything. Andersen replied, "At the moment I do not want to ask for anything, but just to tell your majesty that I am grateful and contented." The other people present reproached Andersen afterward for not having made use of the opportunity to request an increase of his grant (which was something he really did need), for the king had practically put the words in his mouth! He rejected the thought with distaste. It appeared to him to be bad form to request something when one was a guest; if the king wished to do something for him then he would take the initiative himself.[107]

Numerous other contrasts haunted his soul and he knew them. Throughout his life he was the keenest observer and strictest judge of himself. His ambiguity of mind—uncontrolled promptings of emotions juxtaposed with levelheaded self-criticism—contained an enormous conflict that he had to try to embrace. That he was able to carry this additional load was due to a solid grounding of positive, healthy psychological traits: a warm heart, an indestructible will to survive, and a rare confidence in his own genius and fate—the confidence that, by being a good Christian, he invited the intervention of God or Providence. He had a strong, and not unreasonable, feeling that he was under the protection of higher powers. In hours of darkness he could be seized with despair, and in his youth he quietly entered in his diary recommendation to Providence that he be exempted from some of his hard trials.[108] But he would not moan at the forces that led him, and for most of the time he was convinced that Our Lord guided everything for the best.

Just how great his spiritual resistance was and how certain a balance he kept, is exemplified by his humor, his ability to catch the funny side of life, to see what was relative in his own troubles and to raise himself above them. In *The True Story of My Life* he writes that it was this sense of humor that saved him from losing courage when everything seemed bleakest. He had strength enough to look down upon himself with superior self-irony.

CHAPTER 2

Novels, Plays, Poetry, and Travel Books

I Inspiration and Technique

I T is tempting to consider what might have become of Andersen if
he had not escaped from the constricting influence of Odense—a
talented yet unfulfilled eccentric?—a half-crazed character like his
mad grandfather? Then again, what if he had not been rescued in
Copenhagen by such resolute people as Rahbek and Jonas Collin?
There were so many things in life that he was not much good at,
including acting. He could only become a writer.

At first he failed to realize how well-equipped he was. The great
poet's unquenchable thirst to crystallize moods and experiences into
words was his; he too found pleasure in using language, and he
possessed a fertile imagination. Andersen deeply loved poetry; he
wrote fluently and easily; and he possessed a considerable artistic
instinct. He was open to new experiences and knew how to partici-
pate in them. The very turbulence of his early days provided him with
experiences which his fellow poets would have greatly envied if they
had realized how advantageous they were to be; he had, that is, an
abundance of events, moods, and personal problems about which to
write.

In the beginning he thought it was sufficient for a poet to be
enthusiastic and follow the impulses of his imagination; thus, he clung
to "the dogma of immaculate conception untouched by reason," as a
caustic wit once pointed out. [1] There was some truth in this, for he was
highly dependent on his inspiration. [2] Throughout his life he ceaselessly alternated between inspiration and deadness. When a new
work "began to stir within his head," as he expressed it, he often felt a
nervous restlessness that lasted until he had begun to write; he would
then work frenziedly to capture the idea or mood and to give it shape.

61

Afterward came tiredness, or laziness as he called it. When in the mood he could write much in a short time with pleasing results. Several of his most inspired tales were written in quick succession. "The Nightingale" was written overnight, while "The Story of a Mother" came to him in the street and practically wrote itself. While working on the novel *Only a Fiddler* he allowed spontaneous suggestions to decide the course of events and the fates of his characters,[3] and this book, both in his own opinion and in that of the reading public, was one of the most successful of his longer works.

However, he soon discovered that inspiration alone was not enough. With age he grew more critical and he revised and reconsidered more thoroughly his rough drafts. *In Sweden* was the result of a lengthy struggle with language and form, while many of his tales underwent several rewritings before Andersen was satisfied with the result.[4] That irrepressible urge of his to read aloud his new works to all and sundry was, no doubt, in part due to a desire to measure their effect and to test the rhythm and melody of the language; afterwards he would return home to revise his draft.

Nor was he one of those people who make do with what they have already learned and experienced. He read widely, frequently attended the theater, met people from all walks of life, traveled to get fresh impulses, and kept his eyes and ears open wherever he might be. With so many impressions and observations he ought to have had ample material to draw on for his creative writings; and yet he was forever afraid of not having enough. Although his memory was excellent, he mistrusted it, and at an early age he acquired the habit of keeping a diary while traveling. At home he filled notebooks and scraps of paper with notes, random thoughts, and outlines of whatever came to mind. These jottings he kept, often for years, and they were not forgotten. The tales from his later years contain details from notes made twenty or thirty years earlier. Writing was, after all, his way of earning a living, and he "never wasted anything"—as is said of the Finnish woman in "The Snow Queen." A striking example of the thoroughness of his methods is found in "The Muse of the New Century," a fine long lyrical fantasy that is included among his fairy tales. Close examination shows that the fantasy consists of a succession of scattered thoughts and ideas, noted down over the years, and finally integrated into a single whole that gives the impression of having been written in one brief, inspired moment.[5]

Thus Andersen was not merely a literary genius working on inspiration alone; he was also a competent craftsman patiently collecting materials and knowing precisely how to use them.

How could it be that the same writer who paid such careful attention to the details of a fairy tale and who carefully evaluated the relevance of each part to the unity of the whole story, could so often be uncritical and careless when it came to writing plays and composing poems? A failure to understand the requirements of these literary forms would appear to be the answer. He was a narrator, a prose lyricist, and a humorist who was at his best in the small, short form.

There is an impressive range to Andersen's works. That so much could be written in spite of countless journeys, ceaseless social engagements, and a sensitive constitution is most remarkable. To his contemporaries he was by no means just a writer of fairy tales, for he had made a name for himself in almost all the existing genres. A lyric poet and dramatist, as well as a travel writer, in 1835 he tried his hand at the novel and then the fairy tale. Andersen utilized all these literary forms throughout his life. He was still writing lyrical poems in 1875 just a few months before his death, his last play was completed in 1865, and the last travel book in 1866, while *Lucky Peer*, his last novel, was published in 1870. The fairy tales were written right up to 1872.

II *Novels*

While today Andersen's literary fame rests on his fairy tales, in his day the position was different, for it was his first three novels that brought him to the attention of the European reading public: *The Improvisator*, *O.T.*, and *Only a Fiddler* (from the period 1835–1837). Later these were followed by *The Two Baronesses* (1848), *To Be, or Not to Be?* (1857), and *Lucky Peer* (1870). All of them, perhaps with the exeption of *To Be, or Not to Be?* were widely read, in Germany particularly *Only a Fiddler*. Andersen was favorably compared to such European giants as Walter Scott and Victor Hugo.

Of his six novels, the modern reader would receive most pleasure from *The Improvisator*. The hero of this story—begun on Andersen's first journey to Italy in 1833/34—is a poor boy called Antonio who grows up in the slums of Rome. Wealthy patrons, however, provide him with the opportunity to study and, in time, he proves to possess great talent at improvisation. A number of romantic complications take him first to Naples and then to Venice where he meets a girl he has seen in Naples. He falls ill, but her care for him results in them declaring their love for each other. Conveniently, she inherits an estate; the couple then marry.

A modern reader would probably criticize some of the naive episodes, particularly the rather melodramatic and improbable conclusion—an illogical one in that Andersen appears to have forgotten that Antonio was intent on becoming an artist but instead finds ultimate happiness in an attractive bride and an estate in southern Italy. In other respects, however, Andersen achieves success with his hero. Antonio is a poor boy who has to live with his insecurity complex in new and aristocratic surroundings. In addition, he suffers from an inborn nervous fear of his surroundings that makes it difficult for him to believe in his own unquestionable artistic talent and to hold his own against others, including friends and benefactors. This weakness appears, for example, in his relation to the fair sex where he cuts a foolish figure. He would like to love but is afraid of doing so. He dares not allow himself to be tempted by feminine beauty, for he fears the physical attraction. He repeatedly denies, both to himself and to others, his own obvious feelings of love, or he obstinately reinterprets it as brotherly love and invents all sorts of reasons to withdraw from the loved object. A serious illness is needed before finally, practically by surprise, he allows himself to be taken in the arms of his bride; he is an inhibited puritan in full figure—obviously a portrait of Andersen himself.

The character and development of Antonio is the same as the author's, only converted to an Italian setting, and so the book is interesting as an autobiographical document in which Andersen is dressed as one of the theatrical improvisers that he himself saw and heard in Italy. All the problems of the upstart are depicted here: the change of milieu, the troublesome relation with prosperous benefactors, the struggle to be accepted as a rightful member of the upper class and as an artist. But the greatest assets of the novel are the extremely lifelike characters and, above all, the suggestive depiction of the nature and inhabitants of the South. Few writers have been able to make the sunshine and colors of Italy radiate and glow in the manner that Andersen succeeds in doing here. After completing the book the reader is left with the impression that he himself has recently visited this enchanted country.

In the novel with the unusual title *O.T.* the main character also comes from the lower class (he was born in *Odense Tugthus*, i.e., Odense Prison) and works his way up to a position in the upper section of society. The novel has a few well-drawn portraits of minor characters, but in general the figures are very thin and the composition seems amateurish and awkward. The book has hardly any interest for the modern reader.

The third novel, *Only a Fiddler*, deserves closer attention for a number of reasons. The book was published in 1837 and is set in the first half of the nineteenth century, first in Denmark and later in other parts of Europe. There are two main characters, but the author's sympathy for one of them must have carried him away when he gave the novel its misleading title. In reality both characters are equally important in the story. The boy, Christian, whose life occupies the first half of the novel, was born of humble parents in the small town of Svendborg on Funen, and he is the same type as Antonio in *The Improvisator*, only in this case with a gift for playing the violin. His poverty makes it impossible for him to develop his considerable musical talent. He signs on as a deck boy and sails to Copenhagen, which he sees from its good and bad sides (mostly the latter); later he returns to Funen, where, in Odense, he eventually receives proper tutoring in his art. But nothing comes of this, and he ends up as a village fiddler. The reader understands why: throughout the story Christian acts as a cold, wet blanket, a poor fish with no backbone, weak and fearful in face of the realities of life, but filled with a dream of becoming important while being impressed by society, which he wants to enter. From the middle of the book he steps out of the story and only a few glimpses of his sad fate are given. His role as the main character is taken over by Naomi, a Jewish girl whom he knew in his childhood. She is his opposite in all respects: the blood of adventure courses through her veins. She is independent and bold, a wild wench determined to squeeze all she can out of life, no matter the cost—strong where he is weak, an expansive cosmopolitan while he is a cautious home bird. She falls for a handsome, demonic young riding-master of the Byronic breed, and accompanies him into the big, wide world as his mistress. But she is faithlessly and brutally treated and flees from him in bitterness and despair; and after many vicissitudes she ends up in a not particularly happy marriage with a dissolute French marquis in Paris. Thus, both of the main characters have sorrowful fates which are brought out strongly in the concluding pages of the book: Christian, the genius, dies poverty stricken and unnoticed, while Naomi, the woman of the world, obstinately acts out the comedy of life.

It was this novel that activated Søren Kierkegaard to publish his first book, the first lengthy critical examination of Andersen as a writer. This book appeared in 1838, about a year after *Only a Fiddler*.[6] The twenty-five-year-old Søren Kierkegaard already had extensive aesthetic and philosophical studies behind him, and his monograph bears the stamp of the complicated, discursive language and style of the German romantic philosophers (particularly Hegel). The book was such heavy reading that it was claimed that Kierkegaard and Andersen were the only people to have read it from cover to cover. The forty closely printed pages had the characteristic Kierkegaard title: *From the Papers of a person still living, published against his will* with a subtitle, *About Andersen as a novelist with continual reference to his latest work: Only a Fiddler*. Thus, this was to be an examination of Andersen's writings on the basis of the three novels he had published so far; in fact, the monograph deals almost exclusively with *Only a Fiddler*.

Kierkegaard was thorough. After extensive philosophical considerations he discusses the Danish novel and short story of the day: first the novels which were being published under the pseudonym "The author of an Everyday Story" (who was Fru Gyllembourg, mother of J. L. Heiberg). According to Kierkegaard they all had a basic idea, an outlook on life, which was expressed in a positive view of art, beauty, and life itself. He then proceeds to mention the Jutland writer St. Blicher, in whose stories, it is true, he does not find any clearly defined attitude to life but, on the other hand, a fundamentally poetic, although sad, feeling that gives the stories an artistic tone.

With this background Kierkegaard then focuses on Andersen and concludes that he lacks essential requirements for a novelist. Andersen, according to Kierkegaard, has no deep emotions and, even worse, no clearly defined personality (his poetry shows this weakness). In order to expand his personal development he would have to go through "the epic stage," as Kierkegaard calls it; this consists of "a deep and serious embrace of a given reality."[7] By this Kierkegaard implies that by study, observation, and meditation Andersen should experience and see through the trends of his time. But Andersen, with his unrestrained desire to publish, has neither time nor patience for such things. He has only himself to write about. This, however, leads to Andersen's novels taking on "a double light," i.e., they show the poetic picture of imagination but also the author's own experiences and personal reflections. The latter, however, are not integrated into the total artistic picture, for Andersen cannot separate the poetic work from his own person and is therefore unable to create an objective work.

It is unfortunate, says Kierkegaard, that Andersen possesses no firm attitude toward life, for this is a *conditio sine qua non* in a novel. The effect is disastrous in *Only a Fiddler*. True, there is a fundamental theme, namely, that everything great and excellent desiring to burst out is doomed to failure. But in order to be valid as a principal attitude toward life such skepticism must be painstakingly demonstrated through the fate of the main character. But this does not happen in Andersen. "On the contrary, Andersen skips over the actual development, inserts an appropriate interval of time, allows first to be seen the great powers and dispositions, as best he can, and thereafter their damnation." [8] The pessimistic attitude remains as a postulate.

This absense of an attitude toward life gives the novel an unpleasant randomness. The author's anger about the injustice of existence can surface at any time; he encourages and reprimands his characters quite indiscriminately and loses control of the ideas emerging in his mind in connection with the events.

Kierkegaard's final question concerns the depiction in *Only a Fiddler*: is it poetically true, that is, a coherent whole, consistent and credible within the framework of a work of art? Andersen claims that the main character Christian is a musical genius, but no supporting evidence is provided. His childhood musical experiences do not exceed what any child could undergo, and the development of his gifts is not accounted for. His so-called genius dies—why? Because external conditions choke it, and the reader is left to share the author's sadness that this is the way of life. Andersen's theory is as follows: "that genius is an egg in need of warmth, of the stimulations of happiness, otherwise it becomes a wind-egg." [9] But this, says Kierkegaard, is not genius, for genius would break through all difficulties, while Andersen's hero is simply "a sniveler about whom it is maintained that he is a genius." [10] The actual driving force in Christian's life is his vanity: he must obtain the acclaim of the public.

Thus, according to Kierkegaard, Andersen's work contains no firm attitude toward life; it is not objective (i.e., it fails to embody the author's own incidental opinions and feelings); there is no accounting for the genius of the main character and its development; and consequently it is an immature and poorly prepared poetic work.

This is a severe aesthetic evaluation that is difficult to deny. The hardhearted reader could even add more. It is unfortunate that the author allows his title character to sidle into the wings halfway through the book. Kierkegaard does not mention this point but other people had noticed it. One of Andersen's most faithful friends from his earliest days in Copenhagen, old Mrs. Signe Læssøe, wrote to a mutual friend; "There is much beauty in Andersen's latest novel, but I cannot understand how it should all fit together; at first it seems that he considered Christian to be the hero but then Naomi replaces him; can this be done? I believe that no tribunal would accept this as correct; but there are many beautiful details in it." [11] Kierkegaard did not practice music himself for otherwise he would have indicated another particularly weak point: at no stage are we told of the musically gifted Christian practicing scales or of engaging in other technical labors that are the precondition to becoming a competent violinist; we simply hear that he played wonderfully from the first moment he had a violin in his hand—which is technically impossible.

Yet another weakness (Kierkegaard hinted at it and other contemporary critics also noticed it) [12] is Andersen's ill-considered habit of filling out his plot with experiences from his own travels and general comments on this and that, often without a convincing connection between the events or the characters in whose mouth the point is put.

However, despite the criticism the novel was a great success, particularly in Germany, perhaps in the main because of the sentimental plot but probably also because, despite all its weaknesses, it had great poetic merits that Kierkegaard could make nothing of but which, nonetheless, are so great that the novel can also appeal to readers in this century. The description of Christian's childhood is Andersen at his best. The language is clear and precise, the descriptions of situations and nature full of suggestive poetry. What a picture of the south Funen landscape! What power there is in the scenes of pathos, the fire in the neighboring house, the market by the miraculous spring where Christian hopes to be cured of his presumed epilepsy, the frightening Christmas Eve at his half-mad Norwegian godfather's, or the godfather's camouflaged narrative of his life shortly before he hangs himself! The description of young Christian experiencing his surroundings, the portraits of his parents, of Skipper Peter Wik and other common people are convincing in their authenticity and truthfulness. [13] There is precision in the many satirical glimpses of the Copenhagen bourgeoisie and sensitivity in the tragic-naive picture of the prostitute milieu of the capital seen through the inexperienced eyes of the provincial boy. The second half of the book also has excellent figures and episodes. Despite the melodramatic touch there is a convincing authenticity in the Naomi figure, particularly successful in the tragicomic scene where she forces her grandmother, the weakly old countess, to divulge what she knows about her grandchild's origin.[14] The old lady is a monster of comic hypocondria, a self-pitying, highly strung countess who is always dosing herself with medicine, always talking about her complaints, always preparing those around her for her impending death. A passage toward the conclusion of the novel with inspired brevity depicts her type: "In Denmark, on the count's estate the old countess sat surrounded by powders and medicine bottles, even now just as close to death as she was twelve years ago. 'She's tough!' the people of the manor said, 'not even the apothecary can do away with her!' " [15]

Kierkegaard was justified in his criticism of *Only a Fiddler*, but overlooked its good points. It cannot be denied that the novel is heterogenous—which is hardly surprising considering Andersen's own account of how he was writing the novel. In a letter to his fellow poet, B. S. Ingemann (1789–1862) he wrote in February 1837: "In *O.T.* I had a prefixed plan before I wrote a single word; this time, however, I allow the good Lord to look after everything. I have two definite characters, whose lives I will depict; but how they end— well, I must confess—I do not myself know as yet, although the second half is approaching a conclusion—this time I do not write a word without it being given to me, almost forced upon me." [16] The result showed how inadvisable it is for a novelist to leave everything to uncontrolled inspiration.

These first three novels are interesting documents of social conditions in the first half of the nineteenth century and of Andersen's difficult social position. They give a good picture of the conditions that the poor had to live under, and of the relationship between the serving and ruling classes. Notwithstanding the mutual respect and understanding that did exist in many instances between peasant and squire, servant and family, there was a deep gulf between these two segments of society. To cross the gulf was for many impossible. For Andersen this problem was one that he felt he had to write about. These three novels deal in detail with the problems of a poor boy who by his talent rises, or tries to rise, in society. Today's reader cannot fail to notice with a certain distaste how the three main characters try to put as much distance as possible between themselves and their poverty-stricken families. They wish to forget their origins and establish themselves in the world of the bourgeoisie and the aristocracy.

Clearly Andersen held a highly distressing double position toward his own background: [17] he understood these people yet at the same time wished to turn his back on them; his ambitions drove him to make a name for himself among the elite of Europe and by so doing to obtain a much desired world-wide reputation.

Apart from the historical interest, these novels can still please the modern reader through the animated descriptions of situations, people, and scenery. The descriptions of the Italian setting in *The Improvisator* and of the Danish ones in the other two novels have not been surpassed by any later Danish writer. No doubt the melodramatic elements appealed more to the taste of the nineteenth-century reader than to today's.

The Two Baronesses, published in Denmark as well as England in 1848, covers a wide varied and colorful panorama of nature and of people in Denmark around 1840 and includes several extremely well-created characters; one such is the old eccentric female owner of an estate on Funen, a masterpiece of characterization. The minor position now allotted to the social problems is perhaps attributable to Andersen himself being at a greater distance from them.

To Be, or Not to Be? (1857) was Andersen's attempt to come to terms with the heated debate of the period concerning modern science and freethinking, on the one hand, and faith in God and immortality, on the other.[18] The novel tries to prove that the two positions could be combined. The second half of the novel is devoted to a discussion of such a possibility and is practically without interest today, but the first half shows the best of Andersen, with a well-integrated plot, and an original gallery of humorous characters.

Lucky Peer, sometimes translated as *Fortunatus*, is more a short story than a novel. Here again the hero is a poor boy who by his talent, this time as a singer and composer, rises to the top of society. Fortune ivors Peer, who finally attains the greatest of happinesses: to die at the peak of his triumphs. The plot contains little of interest for the modern reader. Yet the minor characters are a feast of original and amusing characters who have helped the story survive beyond its time. Once again the social problem crops up, though in a new and modern shape: some children are born under modest, limiting circumstances while others are born into wealthy homes—why this discrimination? [19]—a question that was to be raised widely in Denmark in later years but in Andersen's work was soon to fade and remain no more than a suggestion. After all, Lucky Peer had had good fortune, just as had the author himself.

That Andersen's novels, despite their literary merits, are little read
today, is attributable to the fact that the novel form was unsuited to
his talents. His strength lay in the precise depiction of an immediate
situation, comic or touching; in the pertinent remark that in a glimpse
reveals a human type or an ordinary human reaction; and in a description of nature or a milieu, the mood of a landscape, of a street or a
room—each in itself excellent but not sufficient to shape a long novel.
Andersen's weakness as a novelist was that he had no deep interest in,
or understanding of, the changing facets of individual mental proces-
ses. To produce a nuanced portrait was not possible for him; his
strength lay in the simplified yet suggestive picture of a type. He also
had difficulties in maintaining the character of a person throughout
the multicomplexity of a long plot and in illuminating it in a variety of
situations. In the novels it is possible to sense that the short form was
his natural domain—a point that his fairy tales amply prove.

III *Plays*

Throughout his life Andersen nurtured an unhappy love for the
theater and, particularly in his younger years, he made great efforts to
convince both the public and the critics that he was a good dramatist.
His most ambitious attempts to attain his ends were the two long
dramas *The Mulatto* and *The Moorish Girl*, both performed at the
Royal Theatre in 1840.

The first play is interesting, for it shows both Andersen's strength
and his weaknesses as a dramatist. He took his theme from a short
story written by Mme. Charles Reybaud, a French authoress, published in *Revue de Paris* in 1838 as "Les épaves" ("The Ownerless
Slaves"). The seventy-page story is set on Martinique in the French
West Indies in about 1720. The social conditions form the backdrop of
the events: the whites and, in part, the Creoles, constitute a wealthy
aristocracy, with blacks forming a proletariat unprotected by law. The
whites' own extensive plantations on which the blacks and mulattos
work as slaves—if they have not run away, to wander in the woods and
mountains as *épaves*. The latter may constitute a threat to the whites,
and at intervals the governor has them captured and sold at the slave
market in St. Pierre, the capital of the colony.

The main characters are Mr. La Rebellière, a brutal white plantation owner, and Donatien, a cultured mulatto, who toward the end of
the story turns out to be a Creole. Between these two are the wife of
the plantation owner, Éléonore, and their young ward, Cécile, who

has just come of age. At the beginning, Éléonore shows the traditional arrogance toward colored people, while Cécile is without any
racial prejudice. Briefly, the story is as follows. Mr. La Rebellière has
to go on a business trip to St. Pierre, and the two women wish to visit a
small property he owns in the mountains. On their way up they are
overtaken by a storm, but find shelter at the house of Donatien,
whose good taste and cultivated manner charms them both. This
meeting marks the beginning of a friendship that develops during the
ladies' stay at their country estate and which results in them both
falling in love with him. On his return from St. Pierre Mr. La
Rebellière discovers his wife's feelings and decides to take revenge.
With the governor's approval he organizes an attack on Donatien's
house, where the owner is arrested together with a group of *épaves* to
whom he has given shelter. He furiously defends himself but is
overpowered and thrown into prison in La Rebellière's house. On the
way there he vainly attempts to commit suicide. As he can be regarded as ownerless he is to be sold on the slave market. By buying
him there La Rebellière will be free to humiliate and mistreat him at
will. During the auction at the slave market both Éléonore and Cécile
make several attempts to prevent the sale, but Donatien is not saved
until Cécile declares that she will marry him, for then, according to
the law, a colored man becomes free through marriage to a white
woman.

Obviously such a story would interest Andersen, for it contains the
clash between despised coloreds and arrogant whites: the action
centers on an inferior person who, after many hardships, is found to
have full value—and this point reminded Andersen of his own fate.
The exotic setting would also have interested him and, moreover, he
knew that exotic subjects were very much in vogue with audiences at
that time.

In his dramatization Andersen closely followed the action of Mme.
Reybaud's short story, but within this framework he naturally had to
make a number of alterations and rearrangements. The time of the
play's setting is not given—perhaps in order not to tie the producer to
a given period color. The hero is not called Donatien but Horatio—
why Andersen chose such a name is difficult to understand; since the
setting is French the main character ought at least to have been called
Horace. Here, moreover, he is not a Creole but a mulatto, an
alteration that Andersen possibly made to sharpen the contrast between Horatio and the whites.

Andersen exploited his source with considerable feeling for the requirements of the theater. His drama, like Mme. Reybaud's story, is excellently constructed and consistently develops to the final scene at the slave market. In other ways, too, Andersen showed good dramatic skill. First, in order to support the audience's impression of the setting, he has given detailed stage instructions. As Frederick Marker has indicated,[20] the furnishings of Horatio's room in the introductory scene are calculated to suggest the hero's breeding, sympathetic background, and intellectual interest in natural history and philosophy. Second, information that in a story could be naturally given as an author's remark is interwoven freely into the dialogue. For example, the first act takes place on the evening of the storm immediately after the arrival of the women at Horatio's house, and via the dialogue the setting is presented: the tropical nature, the relation between the whites and the slaves, and the current situation of each character: Éléonore's marriage, Cécile's recent arrival in Martinique from Paris where she has been brought up—in short, everything that Mme. Reybaud describes in the first pages of her story. Additionally, Andersen presents Horatio's home and his admirable relationship with his slaves, his interests in nature and art. Finally, the seed is sown for later developments in the plot: the rising sympathy that the two women show for the French-cultured mulatto—altogether an excellent background for later developments.

Further on in the play the action has been simplified for good dramatic reasons. For example, Cécile does not visit Horatio's prison (as in "Les épaves"), for on the stage it suffices for her to send a letter via her old Negress slave. In the auction scene at the end, the action is tightened with commendable brevity.

On the other hand, Andersen has expanded and elaborated one of Mme. Reybaud's minor characters, a runaway mulatto slave called Palème, with two monologues in the second act. Moreover, he has added to the action a large ball that Mr. La Rebellière holds in celebration of Cécile's coming of age. This scene immediately follows an episode in the gloomy prison where Horatio has spoken with Cécile's slave and with Palème—a well-calculated effect demonstrating the contrasts between the wretched conditions of the colored slaves and the luxurious life of their white masters.

But Andersen has also made expansions that reveal a less certain instinct for the theater, first and foremost two discursive conversations in the first and third acts about various subjects quite irrelevant for the plot, as well as a number of monologues. Conversations about subjects that do not develop the action are a nuisance in any play; in order to be effective on the stage a monologue should provide a deeper insight into the psyche of the speaker and have convincing poetic precision in its form. At a pinch this might be said to be true of Palème's monologues but scarcely so about those of the other characters.

Finally, there is Andersen's characterization. The sensitive shading that distinguishes Mme. Reybaud's figures is not to be found here. The characters are constructed from just a few conventional traits which, without great variations, are repeated through the five acts and which, moreover, are more than a little sentimentalized. The figures do not grow during the development of events, nor are they given much greater depth. Of Mme. Reybaud's many-sided portrait of Éléonore there is nothing left save her falling in love and her contempt for the coloreds, which Mme. Reybaud allowed to show discretely but which Andersen heavily underlines. The resolute young Cécile in the French novel, who remains cool and efficient in critical situations has, in Andersen's version, only two traits: being in love and sympathy for the coloreds—besides some occasionally muddled philosophical observations that did not come from the French source. The difference between the figures of the two writers is noticeable in the final scene. Their reactions are more sentimental in Andersen's version. When La Rebellière has finally been cheated of his prey by Cécile's proposal of marriage, Mme. Reybaud has her say to Donatien, "Sir, let us go. Will you offer me your arm?" Andersen has the following exchange: "Speak! Will you be free?" Horatio: "Cécile!"

It should be added that her love, as Andersen has shaped it, is without psychological probability and dramatic likelihood; she describes her love as Christian love (act 3, sc. 4); she thanks Horatio for brotherliness (act 4, sc. 2); and declares that she has sisterly feelings for him (act 4, sc. 4)—which cancels out the whole of the eroticism that should be the driving force behind her liberating action.

La Rebellière is concocted according to a very simple recipe; he is a clumsy egoist and materialist, nothing more. He has chosen his wife because she came from a noble family, was wealthy, and had a beautiful shape (act 5, sc. 2), and he has given her everything that money can buy—for then she cannot hate him (act 5, sc. 2). Happiness is gold, he declares (act 4, sc. 2). His stupid brutality toward the slaves, the hissing scorn with which he describes them (act 3, sc. 5), make him a pure caricature, although it cannot be denied that his lines possess the power of bluntness, the rough humor of coarseness, that can be effective on the stage. Mme. Reybaud's sophisticated shading of infamy was not something that Andersen could use.

In "Les épaves" Donatien is presented as a tactful and discreet host, a fine, cultivated, and at the same time a quite unsentimental person. This powerful, uncompromising man who furiously defends himself against the superior force of La Rebellière's soldiers and who attempts suicide because he cannot tolerate the degradation of being sold as a slave becomes, in Andersen's hands, a completely anaemic figure. In act 3, sc. 6, he prettily gives up his love for Cécile with the words: "In God do I own her," and he will make do with that. In act 2, sc. 2, he unexpectedly declares to Palème that his worst enemy is the pride of his heart, a strange piece of self-criticism which remains in the air, as nothing is made of it throughout the rest of the play. It cannot be said that there is a reasonable psychological connexion between his unfailing inoffensiveness and his energetic suicide attempt (act 4, sc. 2).

The sensitiveness and understanding with which Andersen so often depicted ordinary people in his novels is not found in his portrayal of the slaves. Cécile's naive and, in her loyalty, touching old Negress slave in "Les épaves" becomes in Andersen nothing more than a clumsy figure. Her way of expressing herself is neither tasteful nor accurate (see, for example, act 1, sc. 3, and act 3, sc. 1) and in a few places quite out of character. For example, when during the conversation with Horatio in prison she discovers he is the son of Biscuya the squaw, she shouts out jubilantly, "There stands the son of Biscuya! Oh victory! Victory!"—a curious cry from a peasant woman.

There is more substance in the Palème figure as it appears in the two monologues in act 2. His hunger for revenge on his former master La Rebellière and his hunger for women are, in fact, the only feelings that he gives vent to, but they are filled with a not inconsiderable power and with imaginative variations. The prison scene contains several successful lines but also a couple of expressions so clumsy that they destroy the character.

Obviously, Andersen has undertaken a severe simplification as well as a coarsening of the characteristics of the cast he had taken from "Les épaves." This gives them more than a touch of the cliché, an impression that is reinforced by their language. True, there is a host of pictures, comparisons, and metaphors, but they do not grow with any psychological necessity from the characters of the individuals; the lines might as easily be spoken by one person as by another. Often these poetically spiced lines have a merely confusing effect because they seem to be carried by any prevailing wind. There is a wide range of figures and phenomena: Laocoon, Cassandra, Columbus, Moses, desert panthers, the Hindu suttee. In the course of a few lines (act 3, sc. 2) Cécile mentions the queen of Saba, the hieroglyphs, and Beatrice Cenci. In several places the metaphors contradict the author's intention. In Horatio's words, "Our firm will is our suit of feathers, it lifts us from the brink of disaster" (act 3, sc. 6), the "suit of feathers" conflicts with "firm." The old Negress slave says to Horatio in prison (act 4, sc. 7), "I view the harbor of salvation," where there is not a question of coming to rest but, quite the contrary, of a call to action.

Practically every scene contains clumsy and poorly considered expressions, a failing that is surprising when one considers the accuracy of the language of Andersen's fairy tales and even more so when one reads in a letter to one of his oldest friends that he regards his drama as one of the "most carefully prepared" of what he had written so far.[21] The language reveals the failure of Andersen's dramatic figures; it would never have appeared so haphazard if Andersen had experienced his characters from within as independent, distinctive individuals. But he was not able to do so. His weaknesses as a novelist are to be observed in his plays too. In developing situations he lacked the ability to fill out his outlined figures. The creation of a long complicated drama was beyond his talents.

Several of his contemporaries were aware of his shortcomings as a dramatist. The critic and play adviser Molbech was one of them; the famous actress Fru Heiberg (married to J. L. Heiberg) was another. In his advice to the theater board of directors Molbech declared that *The Mulatto* lacked sense, that the actions of the characters were not motivated, and that the lines were only sentimental phrases.[22]

Fru Heiberg agreed with him. Her part was that of Cécile, and she was driven to despair with her role, which she could not take seriously. She thought the poetry in the play was shallow and forced while her own lines were no more than bombastic tattle. She could only go through with her pathetic role by playing it as a kind of parody (a point the audience, fortunately, failed to discover).[23]

Nevertheless, the first performance on 3 February 1840 was rewarded with tumultuous applause and the play was performed no less than twenty-one times up to 11 November 1848, which was a highly successful run in those days. The critics were also enthusiastic about the lyricism (though a few reviewers considered it overdone) as well as the beautiful theme of the drama: the triumph of spirit over the material world—the thought Andersen himself had wished to express. [24] One of the reviewers, however, undertook a detailed comparison between "Les épaves" and *The Mulatto* and concluded that Andersen had taken both plot and characters from Mme. Reybaud, though with certain alterations and additions which were not always too fortunate. The most thorough and understanding critique was written by a talented critic named P. L. Møller who claimed that *The Mulatto* could only be judged fairly if it were regarded as a lyrical drama in the Calderon genre. He praised the lyrical passages but had reservations about the characters.

The contemporary criticism shows how difficult it is to judge the value of a work of art immediately after it has been produced. Andersen himself was certain that the success of *The Mulatto* was due to it being a good play. In reality the reason was that the play satisfied the taste of the period. But tastes change. In the period 1868–1875 it was produced ten times at a private theater in Copenhagen. [25] Since then, however, it has not been performed, and in our century it is difficult to see its good sides. Only the negative criticism of Andersen's contemporaries has been proved right with time. Molbech and Fru Heiberg were more perceptive than most.

The short situation-drama was more suited for Andersen's talents, as for example *I Vetturinens Vogn* (*In the Veturino's Carriage*), a gay portrayal of Danish tourists in Italy, and *Den ny Barselstue* (*The New Birth Room*), which takes place in a Copenhagen house where an author receives a succession of visits from friends who wish to congratulate him on the success of his new play. With its amusing characters and the surprising point of the piece—that the author's play was written by a friend—*Den ny Barselstue* had considerable success and in the present century has been performed many times. In these and other light dramatic pieces the language is very much alive, taken directly from the contemporary reality that Andersen had always been a master in observing and depicting.

IV *Poetry*

Andersen wrote poetry from when he was a schoolboy in Slagelse up to a few months before his death in 1875. Numerous incidental songs, ballads, epigrams for all occasions, commemorative lines on the death of friends, and lyrical poems came through the years from his busy pen. His verse was published in newspapers, magazines, entertainment sheets, and numerous other outlets. Several poems are to be found in his plays and travel books.

The contemporary critics were not always satisfied with them, and posterity has been even more severe. It cannot be denied that Andersen's need to express himself in verse was greater than his talent for this genre. While he showed great care for form when working on his tales, when he wrote verse he could occasionally be rather sloppy. Either he was less critical or his instinct for poetic form was less sure. He himself was somehow aware of the problem. In one of his essays on Andersen[26] Georg Brandes mentions that now and then the old writer would visit him, and on one occasion Andersen said, "I have a feeling you don't like my poems. I know myself that I am not really a lyrical poet; but don't you think that some of them are good?" The young critics's reply is unknown, but the situation must have been rather embarrassing, for Brandes set no great value on the poems, and had both said and written that the fairy tales were the only part of Andersen's work that would survive him. Later critics have been of the same opinion. But such a categorical judgment is unjust. Even though most of Andersen's poems have faded now, it is still possible to collect from the very many a minor nosegay of still fresh flowers.

Most Danes from childhood are familiar with two of Andersen's verse narratives. "The Beech Tree" tells about a tree that is so proud of its branches that it expects to have them eventually sail to distant lands as masts—but the branches end up as fence posts and kindling wood! "The Woman with the Eggs" is a short versified anecdote about the rise and fall of pride:

> There lived a woman beside the fen,
> who, among other things, kept a hen.
> Now, laying eggs is a hen's chief duty,
> and this one daily she laid a beauty;
> to a couple of score the total grew—
> and *that*, thought the dame, was a tidy few!
> She packed them neatly and off she sped
> with the basket balanced upon her head.
> Towards town she trudged with a right good will,
> putting her best foot forward. Still,
> the road was lonely, the distance great,
> and so she had time to speculate
> how much she'd get when her eggs were sold;
> 'twas a nice round sum, if the truth be told.

"Why, dear me, yes," she claimed in glee,
"they'll fetch a whole dollar—and then, you'll see,
two hens I can buy with flesh and feather,
and that'll make three of them altogether!
Each one'll start laying, and it'll be funny
if I can't do another deal worth new money.
So three hens more I must buy—that way
I now shall have six. Of the eggs they lay,
I'll sell off half, and I'll keep the rest
and hatch out chickens; that's much the best.
I'll have quite a poultry-farm, they'll do well—
yes, fowls (just fancy!) they always sell.
Some'll be for laying, and some for sitting—
Lor' bless my soul, how rich I'll be getting!
I'll buy a small sheep and a couple of geese,
and hand over fist my trade'll increase;
What with hens and eggs and feathers and wool
I'll end by having my money-bags full!
I'll purchase a pig, I'll purchase a cow—
maybe I'll even buy two somehow.
There's profit! And, after a year, just peep:
I've house and servants and cattle and sheep.
Then here comes a wooer, my hand he kisses—
and I have a husband and he has a missis!
For he has a farm that is bigger than mine.
I'll grow so superior, haughty and fine
the others'll have to take care what's said;
my goodness, the way I shall toss my head—"
And just as she uttered these words she did it—
splash to the ground her eggs all skidded!
With them her castle of dreams fell flat,
and really there wasn't much harm in that! [27]

This is a moral tale with a cheerful picture of human frailty.

Just as successful are Andersen's short, touching, and humorous scenes from everyday life, such as "A Study from Nature," with its masterly brief picture from the small town: a narrow yard with only one gooseberry bush and with the sheets hung up to dry in the sun; the small children lying on a bolster enjoying life in the sunshine, their messy, half-eaten bread and butter in their hands, melting when they fall asleep; the foolishly proud cockerel craning its neck and crowing; and over everything there is the sunshine and satisfaction with a humble way of life.

Andersen also wrote children's verse, but strangely enough not

very many. One of them is "Little Svend's Comments on the
Weather":

> This weather seems so very silly,
> Changing its mind quite willy-nilly.
> Now it's thawing, the streets are streaming,
> Now it's freezing, we'll soon be skating.
> Then a snow-storm whirls along,
> So we'll need our fur-hats on.
>
> The sparrows all seem blown away,
> Even the ice on the pond won't stay.
> The thin-ice breaks with proper cracks,
> And old folk keep falling on their backs.
> Now a down-pour, now clear blue sky,
> Such silly weather, I wonder why?
>
> But I'll not go round complaining.
> If there's frost I'll go out skating,
> If it thaws then I'll wear waders,
> And walk deep in muddy waters.
> Sleet and snow-storm; let them come!
> I'll be out there having fun!

It would be difficult to guess that this little jewel of good spirits was in
fact written just a few months before the poet's death.[28]
    The more serious poems were less often as satisfactory in
Andersen's hands. His love poetry cannot be compared with corre-
sponding poetry written by other Danish poets (such as Christian
Winther (1796–1876), Emil Aarestrup (1800–1856), or Holger
Drachmann (1846–1908), but a few of them have maintained a certain
popularity, as for example, the following two:

> Two brown eyes I did lately see—
> a home and a world lay there for me.
> With goodness and childlike peace they shone;
> I'll never forget them while life goes on.
>
> There is a legend wonderful to tell:
> Each mussel shell
> that deep within the salty sea doth lie,
> once it hath formed its pearl, must surely die.
> O love, thou art the pearl my breast did pray for—
> and now with life must pay for!

A few of the serious poems were composed in those particularly
fortunate moments when inspiration brought about the intimate
union of thought and form, characteristic of great poetry. One of
these is "A Poet's Last Song," written not in old age, as could be
assumed, but thirty years before his death:

> Bear me but hence, thou mighty Death,
> to where the souls abide me!
> Forward I've gone with fearless breath
> the way that God did guide me.
> The songs I sang, O God, were thine—
> unguessed the wealth that filled them;
> 'Twas little art they held of mine;
> like bird on bough I trilled them.
>
> Farewell, red rose of fragrant breath,
> farewell, ye dear ones yonder!
> Bear me but hence, thou mighty Death,
> though here 'twas good to wander.
> Thanks be to God for all he gave
> and ceaseth not from sending.
> Fly, Death, o'er Time's eternal wave
> where summer waits unending!

Another poem is "The Dying Child," which he wrote in one of his
darkest hours of schooling when he was twenty-one years old: [29]

> Mother, I'm so tired, I want to sleep now:
> Let me fall asleep and feel you near,
> Please don't cry—there now, you'll promise, won't you?
> On my face I felt your burning tear.
> Here's so cold, and winds outside are frightening,
> But in dreams—ah, that's what I like best:
> I can see darling angel children,
> When I shut my sleepy eyes and rest.
>
> Mother, look, the Angel's here beside me!
> Listen, too, how sweet the music grows.
> See, his wings are both so white and lovely,
> Surely it was God who gave him those.
> Green and red and yellow floating round me,
> They are flowers the Angel came and spread.
> Shall I, too, have wings while I'm alive, or—
> Mother, is it only when I'm dead?

> Why do you take hold of me so tightly,
>   Put your cheek to mine the way you do?
> And your cheek is wet, but yet it's burning—
>   Mother, I shall always be with you . . .
> Yes, but then you mustn't go on sighing;
>   When you cry I cry as well, you see.
> I'm so tired—my eyes won't stay open—
>   Mother—look—the Angel's kissing me!

It is noteworthy that this description is quite free of sentimentality despite the pitifulness of the child's death: the despair of the mother is not described, only hinted at, through the child's surprise about her tears. In its simplicity this poem is a pearl of condensed atmosphere.

Also quite unsentimental is the gentle tone of joy and veneration in the short Christmas song published in his 1832 collection of poems.

> Child Jesus in a manger lay
> Yet Heaven knew His power
> His bed was here among the hay
> While darkness draped his bower.
> Above the stall the star stood still
> And the ox knelt down before His will.
> Halleluja, Child Jesus.

> Each saddened soul
> Be glad and bright,
> Your heavy load will now depart,
> In David's town was born this night
> A child to cheer each fearful heart.
> To reach this child must be our goal
> And be a child in heart and soul.
> Halleluja, Child Jesus.

In these simple lines the setting—the humble stable, the animals around the child, the star in the heavens—and the consolation that this insignificant event bears for the Christian reader have blended together into a picture of unique musical clarity.

The most famous of Andersen's poems, however, are the two patriotic songs, "Jutland Between Two Seas," a poetic picture of the large Jutland peninsula stretching out from the European mainland with the North Sea on one side and The Baltic on the other, and "In Denmark I Was Born." The latter was written in 1850 under the

influence of the war with Germany and is an enthusiastic homage to
the poet's native country:

> In Denmark I was born, and there 'tis homely,
> there clings the root whence all my being flows.
> O Danish tongue, your tones are soft and comely,
> none but a mother's voice could soothe like those.
> > You smiling Danish strand,
> > where Viking barrows muster,
> while round them orchards bloom and hop-vines cluster,
> 'tis you I love—Denmark, my native land!
>
> Oh, where is summer's boon in flowery meadow
> more golden than beside this open strand?
> Where falls on moonlit clover-field a shadow
> so fair as in the beech's native land?
> > You smiling Danish strand,
> > where Dannebrog is flying—
> God-gifted flag, God give you fame undying!
> 'tis you I love—Denmark, my native land!
>
> You mastered England once and overran it,
> ruled all the North—but now men say you wane;
> so small a land—yet up and down our planet
> still ring the song and chisel of the Dane.
> > You smiling Danish strand,
> > plough turns up golden treasure;
> God gild your future, too, in equal measure!
> 'tis you I love—Denmark, my native land!
>
> O land where I was born, to me so homely,
> where clings the root whence all my being flows,
> whose accents are my mother's, soft and comely—
> no music ever stirred my heart like those.
> > You smiling Danish strand,
> > that swans have built their nest in,
> green islands that my heart finds perfect rest in,
> 'tis you I love—Denmark, my native land!

As can be seen, the poem consists of a series of partly unconnected
outbursts of feeling, each of which gives a piece of Danish nature or
Danish history, a mosaic linked by a kind of double refrain: each verse
concludes with " 'tis you I love," and in the middle of each verse
comes the same line, "you smiling Danish strand." But the unity of

the poem also lies in its basic feeling: the poet's love for Denmark. It is here that he belongs, which is clearly emphasized at the beginning of the first verse and at the conclusion of the final verse as a frame around the picture of Denmark: the fertile countryside with apple gardens and clover fields, and the beach which is never far away. Here the Dannebrog waves, the Danish banner, "God-gifted," for the story has it that when the Danish king in 1219 set out on a crusade across the Baltic to Estonia he had to engage in fierce fighting with the Estonians, and when the battle was at its height, the red banner with the white cross fell down from heaven as a decisive encouragement for the Danish warriors. The Danes were victorious, and the banner of the cross became from then on the symbol of the Danish Kingdom. Verse 3 recalls two other events from Danish history: in the eleventh century the Danish king ruled over all of Scandinavia and England; now, however, Denmark is a small and weak country, but throughout the whole world there are Danes whose song and chisel strokes can be heard—the reference to "song" is obscure, but the "chisel-strokes" undoubtedly suggest Thorvaldsen, the Danish sculptor known throughout Europe and an elder contemporary and friend of Andersen's. "The golden treasure" is a golden horn, originating in about 400 A.D., that was found in a field in southern Jutland in 1639 by a peasant when he was ploughing; a second horn was found at about the same spot one hundred years later (they were regarded as Denmark's greatest antiquarian treasures, but were both stolen from the museum in Copenhagen in 1802 and melted down—an event which gave occasion to Oehlenschläger's romantic program-poem "Guldhornene," written in the same year).

This short selection of Andersen's best poems should be sufficient to provide a positive answer to his own worried question to Georg Brandes whether the young critic could not feel that at least some of his poems were good.

V   *Travel Books*

Andersen's travel books deserve to be far better known than they are, for, next to his tales, they are the most animated and engaging of his works. They are interesting for several reasons. First, there is the historic perspective of Europe in the middle of the nineteenth century; a changing Europe where peasant and prince still existed while the new civilization of technology was making itself felt. Second, these books contain all the positive qualities of good reporting. The reader travels with a man who experiences everything with all of his senses alert and who understands how to communicate these experiences with imagination and cheerfulness.

Andersen was the ideal traveler. He loved movement, changes, constantly varying surroundings, the strange and the new; and he was granted the possibility of satisfying this passion year after year. "To travel is to live," he claimed.[30] He disliked remaining for long periods in Denmark, where everything seemed so limiting. And what would become of his fame if he did not travel and promote it a little? He had to introduce himself and encourage interest in his books.[31] Moreover, he had to travel to obtain the material he needed for his creative writing. In Denmark he had found what he could use in a decade, and so it was necessary for him to travel to find more.

He thus became a cosmopolitan in the little pond of Danish literature. He traveled further afield than any other Danish writer of his time: through most of Europe, even Greece, the Balkan Peninsula, Spain, and Portugal; he set foot in North Africa (from Spain) and Asia Minor, he could even have gone to America and would probably have done so if the Atlantic had not been in the way.

There is something of an art about traveling and not everybody possesses that art. You need to be practical and thrifty (Andersen was both) and have curiosity and keen eyesight. The poor tourist soon tires, then starts reading a paper. The real traveler stretches out his neck so as not to miss a thing. Andersen never tired of seeing, and his eyesight never dulled. Of course, he was far more than a tourist; he was also a poet and a writer—a poet, that is, who saw better than others, who could catch the comic or pathetic in a chance situation, the unusual in a landscape, or something interesting in the people who happened to pass by. The ordinary traveler notices a man at the station or in the street and thinks to himself, "Hmm, what an unusual face!" then walks on, preoccupied with other things. With Andersen the impression would be seized and then allowed to continue an existence within his imagination, to unfold later in pictures of humor, beauty, and perspective. He was always experiencing something, for he seemed to have a special ability, as some people do, to arrive at a place exactly at the moment something interesting was taking place; or was the secret that he noticed what other people walked right past? Once when he was at Admiral Wulff's, a home he had regularly visited from his early days in Copenhagen, Andersen was relating one of his anecdotes when the gruff old salt, scratching his hair in comic despair, exclaimed, "It's a lie, a downright bloody lie! That kind of thing never happens to any of us!" [32]

Then Andersen was a writer who always had to be on the lookout for fresh material. He was untiring, even slavish, in recording his experiences and what others had told him.[33] Despite his excellent memory he wanted to be certain of not slipping up when exploiting material for literary purposes. This genuine ability to notice and experience, to sense and reproduce a certain atmosphere was what helped make his travel books so popular among his contemporaries and helps make them readable to this day. People have often called him a journalist, but he cannot be compared with the expert journalists of today, for he was usually quite unprepared before visiting a foreign country; in fact, he is akin to the modern hurried reporter. He saw people and things and recorded what he saw. The reader will not find any information about the political and social conditions of the countries he visited. Andersen grew up in the Denmark of absolute monarchy, where all social problems were dealt with by the king and his council, and he lived in a society where interest was focused on the higher values of poetry. Nor do his characterizations of the people he encountered or saw on his journeys have great depth to them. His strength lay in the sharp yet external observation, following which he allowed his imagination to substitute for any deeper knowledge concerning what he saw.

He wrote no less than five travel books. The first, about his first journey to Germany, was entitled *Rambles in the Romantic Regions of the Hartz Mountains, Saxon Switzerland, etc.* (1831; English translation, 1848); the second was about his long journey as far as Asia Minor, *A Poet's Bazaar* (1842; English translation, 1846); the third dealt with his visit to Sweden in 1849, *In Sweden* (1851; English translation, 1852); the fourth concerned his trip to Spain, *In Spain* (1863; English translation, 1864); and, finally, the short and somewhat indifferent *A Visit to Portugal 1866* (1868; English translation, 1870).

The last two travel books have recently been retranslated into English, but the first three are no longer available—which is a great pity. His youthful book about Germany is full of evocative or humorous descriptions of towns, people, and scenery. *In Sweden* is a vast multicolored canvas of that extensive and distinctive Scandinavian country, while *A Poet's Bazaar* is Andersen's masterpiece of travel reporting. Some sections are of minor interest; yet there are a number of descriptions that remain fresh to this day, such as the marvellous characterization of the German towns, the account of Andersen's first ride on a railway, the crossing of the Brenner Pass by coach in the deathly stillness of a cold winter afternoon and evening, the complicated journey by *vetturino* down through Italy, the voyage across the Mediterranean, and visits to Greece, Constantinople, and the Balkans, which for the North Europeans were practically unknown countries. That *A Poet's Bazaar* has not been retranslated in this century is indeed astonishing. It is true that the first section of *In Spain* is written with an exuberant, inventive sense of humor. But it is surprising that English editions of these less impressive books on Spain and Portugal have appeared, while his better travel books are ignored.

CHAPTER 3

The Fairy Tales

I *Tales for Children*

EVEN if he had not written the fairy tales Andersen would have become a famous writer, both in his own time and today—at least in Denmark. But the tales proved to be his crowning glory—an ironic twist of fate, since this writer who was so hungry for fame had no inkling at first that they were to take his name farther than anything else.

The retelling of folktales or the writing of new ones in the same form was by no means a new interest; European writers had been doing so for centuries, while in Denmark Oehlenschläger and Ingemann, poets of a slightly older generation, had both written in that genre. Why should not a young ambitious writer follow suit, particularly when he had always loved this poetry of the common people? Actually, nobody was closer to it than Andersen, the child of the common people. As early as 1829 he had made his first attempt at the form with "Dødningen" ("The Ghost"), which concluded the volume of poems he published in January 1830. In the introduction he wrote, "As a child my greatest pleasure was to listen to tales. A great number of them still live in my memory, and some of these are not very well known, if they be known at all. Here I retell one of them; if it is favorably received I will then take up some more and perhaps produce a cycle of Danish folktales." [1] However, the Copenhagen critics did not encourage the author to continue with this form; quite understandably so, considering the uncertain style and the repeated inclusion of quotations from Andersen's extensive reading and hints of all sorts of literary phenomena that were poorly fitted to a folktale.

Perhaps he was aware of this himself; at least he put aside his plans for some time. Toward the end of 1834, when he had nearly finished

The Improvisator, he took up the subject again. "Now I am beginning to write some "Fairy Tales for Children," he wrote in a letter to a friend on New Year's Day, "I want to win the next generations, you see!" A month later he wrote much the same to his friend and fellow poet Ingemann, adding, "I have written them completely as I would tell them to a child." [2]

Here Andersen was being totally original. As to how that idea came to him, he himself says nothing definite; but in his book about Andersen Edvard Collin writes that he clearly remembered how the writer would often entertain the children of the many houses that he regularly visited by telling them "stories which he partly made up on the spur of the moment, partly borrowed from well-known fairy tales; but whether the tale was his own or a retelling, the manner of telling it was entirely his own, and so full of life that the children were delighted. He, too, took delight in letting his humor run free. He spoke continually with plenty of phrases that children used, and gestures to match. Even the driest of sentences was given life. He didn't say, 'The children got into the carriage and then drove away,' but, 'So they got into the carriage, good-bye Daddy, good-bye Mummy, the whip cracked, snick, snack, and away they went, giddy up!' People who later heard him reading aloud his tales would only be able to form a faint impression of the extraordinary vitality with which he told them to children." [3] Collin observes that it was Andersen's success with children, and also the eavesdropping of adults, that gave him the encouragement to publish the first fairy tales. Thus Andersen found the magic stone where he was least expecting it. He was very fond of children but had no wish to be a children's poet. Nevertheless, it was his young audience that gave him the unconventional form of narration that he needed, and opened for him the road to fame.

But it is one thing to tell a story to a living audience and another to put it into written form. When publishing the first fairy tales Andersen had to face the difficult task of transferring the liveliness of the spoken word to the word on the page. It was necessary to create a new style of written language, and the triumph of his genius was that he could do so, and do so straight away. That first slim volume, from the spring of 1835, indicated, without Andersen being aware of it, a turning point in his authorship, and a turning point in the history of Danish prose.

His achievement was twofold: first, he put into print spoken language with all its inconsistencies of logic and syntax; second, he removed all those words and expressions, particularly the abstract ones, that only adults used. How thoroughly he carried this out is made apparent by comparing "The Ghost" (1829) with its reworked version entitled "The Traveling Companion" (1835).[4]

In the same year as the publication of the first volume of fairy tales Andersen sent out a second volume, but it would be unfair to say that the Copenhagen critics were responsible for this fresh literary initiative.[5] The most respected literary periodical in Copenhagen did not even mention the tales, and of the two critics who did trouble to review them, one believed that it was an impossible task to set colloquial language onto the printed page, while the other critic openly stated that children ought not to have such literature in their hands; it was impossible through fairy tales to instill into children the proper beneficial knowledge concerning nature and mankind—this would only lead to filling their imaginations with fantastic opinions. According to this critic, children will find little edification in Andersen's fairy tales:

At least nobody will be able to claim that the child's sense of propriety will be improved by reading about a princess who rides in her sleep on the back of a dog to a soldier who kisses her . . . or that the child's sense of decency will be developed by reading about the farmer's wife who, while her husband is away, entertains the parish clerk alone . . . or that the child's respect for human life is increased by reading about how Big Klaus clumps grandmother or how Little Klaus kills Big Klaus, narrated as casually as if a bull were being clumped on the head. The tale of the princess on the pea appears to this reviewer not only to be indelicate but also indefensible, for the child will imbibe the false impression that ladies of high rank must be terribly thin-skinned.

Ingemann was less critical, but even he thought that Andersen could make better use of his time, and he was not the only one to reach this conclusion. Others, though, were more perceptive. The very first volume of tales caused H. C. Ørsted, the physicist, to pronounce the now well-known judgment that if *The Improvisator* made Andersen famous, then the fairy tales would make him immortal. Even Heiberg, much to Andersen's astonishment, valued them higher than the novels and also declared that the fairy tales would give their author the highest place in the world of literature.[6]

Andersen did not know who to believe. Naturally he thought that the critics were stupid, but he also thought that his friends were mistaken. To him the tales were only entertainment, charming trifles without much literary value. That was not how he intended to win his laurels. But since children wanted them and he needed the money, and, moreover, because he enjoyed telling fairy tales, he decided to continue. Thus in the years that followed he published more—when, that is, he was not engaged in other, and in his opinion, more important undertakings, such as his novels and plays.[7]

Andersen had begun by retelling tales that he had heard in his childhood on Funen:[8] "The Tinder Box," "Little Klaus," and "The Princess on the Pea"; but the fourth one, "Little Ida's Flowers," which concluded the first volume, was more or less an original story. Soon he was inventing more than retelling. "The Traveling Companion," "The Wild Swans," and "The Swineherd" are folktales, while "The Naughty Boy" was an idea he got from a short poem written by the classic Greek lyricist Anacreon. "The Emperor's New Clothes" is an old Spanish story, "The Rose Elf" reproduces an Italian folksong, while "The Flying Trunk" has its motif from *The Arabian Nights*. Of the 156 tales printed in his collected works Andersen claims that only nine are retellings: "The Tinder Box," "Little Klaus," "The Princess on the Pea," "The Traveling Companion," "The Wild Swans," "The Garden of Eden," "The Swineherd," "Simple Simon," and "What Father Does is Always Right." The remainder are his own inventions.

No matter the origin of the tales, Andersen's young audience was delighted. The concrete, direct narrative was brilliantly adapted to their range of comprehension; children have always enjoyed folktales, and the other stories are equally simple in plot and theme and take place among persons and in settings that children know—or did in those days.

Andersen was long in realizing the value of his fairy tales, and for a number of years regarded them as sideline compositions. But their unparallelled success finally helped change his mind. They were read and admired not only in Denmark but in other countries, and by an increasing number of adults. It was this adult audience that eventually convinced him that Ørsted and Heiberg were right, and that he, somewhat against his will, had created a completely new literary form that was as good as any of the conventional forms of writing, and which was completely his own. He realized that it was possible to use the tales to express adult thoughts for an adult reading public. In a letter to Ingemann in 1843 he wrote:

I believe that I have now found out how to write fairy tales! The first ones I wrote were, as you know, mostly old ones I had heard as a child and that I usually retold and recreated in my own fashion; those that were my very own,

such as "The Little Mermaid," "The Storks," "The Daisy," and so on,
received, however, the greatest approval and that has given me inspiration!
Now I tell stories of my own accord, seize an idea for the adults—and then tell
it for the children while still keeping in mind the fact that mother and father
are often listening too, and they must have a little something for thought.[9]

From now on his little volumes no longer had the title "Fairy tales
Told for Children" but simply "Fairy Tales."

II   *Tales For Everyone*

Thus he was now writing for both the children and the adults. This
was two-level composition in Andersenian terms: the language and
the fairy tale setting he kept, but the thoughts behind them were for
the listening parents. This creative process was, however, not completely new. Tales as early as "The Little Mermaid" and "The
Goloshes of Fortune" were not primarily intended for children,[10] and
in the children's tales "a little something for the thoughts" was
scattered about that could scarcely be comprehended by children.
However, after 1843 Andersen deliberately aimed at an adult audience. Children certainly enjoy both "The Snow Queen" and "The
Nightingale" as well as many others, but they can hardly plumb the
depths of these stories; while tales such as "The Bell," "The Story of a
Mother," or "The Shadow" are just not understood by young listeners. The simple, pseudochildish narrative style is no more than an
intriguing disguise, a refined naiveté permitting irony or seriousness
to have a stronger hold.
   Andersen had gradually developed this original form of telling
tales, and reached perfection in the years following 1843. All his
masterpieces—such as "The Sweethearts," "The Ugly Duckling,"
"The Fir Tree," "The Little Match Girl," "The Shirt Collar," and so
on—came into being during this period. In 1849 his entire production to date of fairy tales was published in a large, collected edition: a
tribute to the artistic capacity of the not yet forty-five-year-old writer.
   Yet he was not finished with the tales. In 1852 he published two
more collections, though with a new title. He now called them
"Stories"—he needed a more comprehensive title and he had his
reasons.[11] The two collections did contain more fairy-talelike descriptions, such as "The Goblin at the Grocer's" and "It's Perfectly True,"
but there was much more as well: "The Story of the Year" is a long,
lyrical nature painting; "A Good Temper" is a cheerful causerie;

"Heartbreak" and "She was No Good" are situations and fates from real life; "In a Thousand Years' Time" presents a futuristic vision; and "Beneath the Willow-Tree" is a short story. Moreover, Andersen had earlier tried his hand at reporting and lyrical pictures. *Picture Book without Pictures* (1839) is comprised of a number of scenes and experiences from both near and far, pathetic, touching, humorous, ironic—brief tales told by the moon to the lonely young artist up in his garret. It was to creative writing in this genre that Andersen returned in 1852, and during the last twenty years of his life he wrote many similar descriptions in addition to a number of narratives of the sort we would nowadays call short stories. Still, he did not completely discontinue telling fairy tales; beginning in 1858 he called his collections "Tales and Stories," a fortunate title, for he was thus able to place tales and nontales side by side, and had no need to differentiate between the two groups, which anyway would have been pointless. There are short stories that are completely realistic and others that also have a fairy-tale touch about them. Whether the latter are called tales or not is only a question of taste. What they have in common is the short form that always suited Andersen best of all. Numerous sketches first published separately in periodicals and almanacs were included in his complete works among the fairy tales on the simple ground that they were short.

On the whole, his writings after 1852 do not come up to the level of his masterpieces from the preceding decades. But there is much that is still remembered and deserves to be so. All Danes, old and young, at least know "Simple Simon" (also called "Clod Hans)" and "What Father Does is Always Right," both retellings of folktales, and "The Snow Man," and many certainly know "The Marsh King's Daughter," "Soup from a Sausage Stick," and "The Beetle." Among the now lesser-known stories comes "The Ice Maiden," that magnificent long fairy tale set in Switzerland and concerned with frail human beings up against the strong, dangerous powers of nature. "The Wind Tells the Story of Valdemar Daa and His Daughters" is a bizarre tale of fate told to the continual accompaniment of the whine of the wind. "Lovely" gives an unforgettable picture of the talkative, unintelligent mother-in-law. "Something to Write About" is the story of the poor young man who wants to be a poet by Easter and then live from his poems, but who, alas, lacks the ability to find something to write about. "Auntie" tells about an old spinster who had regularly visited the theater for fifty years and whose knowledge of life was taken entirely from the stage. "The Dryad" is a brilliant and originally shaped description of the Paris World's Fair in 1867. "The Great Sea-Serpent" describes the laying of the telegraph cable beneath the Atlantic.

Several of these tales were written when Andersen was well over sixty, but his age does not show. He retained a freshness of mind until the very last illness took away his strength.

III   The World of the Folktales

At this stage it is worthwhile to consider in greater detail the development of Andersen's fairy tale. First, we must return to our earlier comment, that during the eighteenth and nineteenth centuries Europe was divided into two social layers: the upper or ruling class and the lower or serving class. The difference between them was not only an economic one. It was also a difference between conditions of life and conceptions of life. The surroundings of the upper class were well-protected homes and streets, theaters and books. Their conception of the world was based on mechanical physics, that is, their universe was considered to be an enormous machine, an interplay of impersonal forces functioning according to the eternal laws of physics. The common mass of people had quite a different view. Around them, particularly in the country districts, was remorseless nature; immediately outside their doors was the anguish of darkness; their days were drudgery. They knew nothing about world mechanics. Their world was one of separate phenomena. Their universe was peopled with forces acting and reacting as arbitrarily as human beings. The storm was no mechanical phenomenon, nor was the sea, the trees, the earth and its fruit. While trolls, nisser, elves, and ghosts perhaps did not always have great influence on everyday life, they were still an important part of the common man's range of ideas. This way of experiencing life and nature was characterized by the upper class as superstition, a rather condescending term serving to show that the ruling cultured class did not know or understand the living conditions of the common people.

Furthermore, the culture of the upper class was firmly based on the written word: the traditions from Greek and Roman poetry and philosophy that were continued in Italy, Spain, France, England, and the Germany of the eighteenth century. The common people did not have a written literature; instead they had their own oral tradition (fairy tales, folksongs, legends) that was certainly as old as the written literature of the aristocracy. Behind the fairy tales lay a life of hundreds, even thousands of years. They were the common people's entertainment in an often harsh and drab existence. They took place in a world with which the listener was familiar even though the events were more jumbled and varied. Moreover, the listener was encouraged to hear about the possibility of extrication from a harsh existence. The brave young man's courage, perseverance and cunning help him to win a princess and half a kingdom. The listeners found comfort and strength in the thought that even if they themselves could not obtain the great prize there were some who could. Thus the tales both expressed their fears and gave them their hope.

The fairy-tale audience was by no means sophisticated: action, surprise events, and a happy ending were all that they needed. So the crude tales rarely had the polish of works of art.

Andersen had been brought up in this ancient universe, he knew the world of these people, their poetry, and had felt its truth. Then came his grammar school education. His entry into the world of the bourgeoisie in Copenhagen removed him from the childhood environment and placed him in the cultured upper class. This ascent was his weakness—he was an outsider—yet it proved to be his strength. When he first came to Copenhagen with that famous pitiful fourteen *rigsdaler* and the small bundle of clothes, he was also carrying something far more precious: the spiritual luggage that was going to make his fortune.

IV *Recreating Folktales*

Andersen was by no means the first writer to introduce the tales of the people to the literary aristocracy. In 1697 Perrault published his *Contes de ma mère d'Oye*, a small collection of tales of a popular origin, and other writers followed suit in the eighteenth century. For example, in Germany *Volksmärchen der Deutschen* by Musäus (1782–1785) was widely read. The romantic movement at the turn of the century provoked interest in the hitherto ignored (not to say despised) lower classes, and learned people started searching for folklore treasure. The folktales collected in the German countryside by the Grimm brothers were one result of this scholarly interest. But Andersen was no folklorist, he was no student walking out from his library to discover a new world full of curious beliefs and superstitions. He himself came from the common people. To him their world was not something that needed to be learned; it was his own world and had been so since birth. So the luggage that the youth from

Odense had with him was something that other poets of the day did not, and could not, have: a new literary form, the fairytale, or perhaps better, the fairy short story. Moreover, he was bringing something of greater importance, a new world, one of quite different people, natural laws, and even morals from those the bourgeoisie of Copenhagen was used to. Andersen was able to plant a new tree in the garden of Danish literature, a tree with strange blossoms and wonderfully fresh fragrance.

What did Andersen do to the folktale? He changed it; he had to. After all, he had to tell the tale to well-reared Copenhagen children, so much retouching was necessary. In a note to "The Swineherd" Andersen says that it could not with "decency" be retold in the manner he had heard it as a child, for it was not for delicate ears.[12] There were other reasons why he had to change them. The way they were told among the common people would not satisfy cultivated literary taste. Admittedly we do not know much about the tales as Andersen heard them as a child, but they would seem to have been similar in style to those recorded by the Grimm brothers as well as by Danish folklorists. As mentioned earlier, these tales are far from literary masterpieces. As a rule their composition is rather planless and haphazard; incidents lack practical or psychological plausibility (for example, the supernatural works quite arbitrarily), characters are no more than clichés, and there are no descriptions of the external surroundings in which they live and act. In short, everything that an educated literary public would expect was missing: clarity of composition, logical coherence of plot, nuanced characters, a clear picture of the environment and setting, and, underlying everything, some basic idea. Moreover, in a literary fairy tale the supernatural events should be ruled by a kind of inner consistency.

If Andersen was to have any hope of his writings being accepted within the world of literature, in short, if he wanted to create a Danish *Kunstmärchen*, then he had to meet these requirements. He did so from the very first tales, in part, perhaps, because he had an adult audience in mind from the very beginning, and, possibly because he realized the need to write for an educated public.

V   Retellings of Folktales

"The Tinder Box," the first of his retellings, is a literary pearl.[13] The main character is a young soldier who, on returning from the war, meets an old witch who asks him to climb through a hole in a tree, and then descend to a cave beneath it where he can fetch all the money he can carry. The money is guarded by three large dogs, but the soldier is not to worry, for all he has to do is to lift them off and put them on her apron and they will not harm him. All she wants him to get for her is an old tinderbox left by her grandmother. However, when he returns, the witch refuses to tell him what she wants the tinderbox for, so he cuts off her head and keeps the box. He proceeds to a fine town where he soon spends all his money. By chance however, he discovers that by striking a light on the tinderbox he can bring before him the three dogs and that they can fetch him as much money as he wants from the cave beneath the tree. Moreover, he finds that the dogs can perform other services for him, such as fetching the lovely princess who has been locked up in a copper castle so that nobody might see her. One of the dogs brings her at night and then returns her, but in the morning she tells her family that she has had a curious dream about a dog and a soldier. The king and queen are suspicious, so a lady-in-waiting is told to sit up and keep watch. By this means the soldier is discovered, put in prison, and is sentenced to be hanged. But with the help of the tinderbox he escapes this fate; he summons the three dogs, who dispatch the king and queen and the whole court. The soldier then marries the princess.

This story follows the usual pattern of the folk fairy tale: the brave young hero comes through many trials and finally wins the princess and the kingdom. But what a difference there is from the haphazard form of the folktale! In Andersen's version the plot is intensified as much as possible. Events follow each other in quick succession. There are no unnecessary words. There is no beating about the bush when the witch tackles the soldier about fetching the tinderbox nor when she refuses to tell him what she will do with the strange object: the matter is settled immediately. No sooner have the dogs dispatched the king and queen and court than the wedding takes place. However, the greatest difference lies somewhere else. The folktale does not make much out of setting or characters, while in Andersen the story is full of details that bring people and situations closer and make them more familiar: the king and queen drink tea at breakfast, the soldier smokes a pipe, and the witch's grandmother can forget things. Moreover, the persons are distinct individuals with traits we all recognize. An additional attraction lies in the incredibly short space within which the characterization is drawn. A stroke and the character is alive. The soldier's friends are very fond of him when he is rich, but they cannot manage all the stairs when he is poor and is

98

living in an attic. When the queen hears of the nighttime visit her comment, "That's a pretty tale, if you like!" is enough for us to recognize her, as too is the king's, "I won't be tossed," when the dogs are hurling the courtiers to their deaths.

As for the soldier himself: when he hears that there is a pretty princess at the castle he immediately asks, "Where is she to be seen?" But alas she is not to be seen, for she is locked up. "I'd like to see her!" thought the soldier but, "of course, he could not possibly get leave to." To indicate more in so short a space would be impossible: a brave soldier, both inquisitive and fond of women, and bored to boot, who does not seem likely to be stopped by something being forbidden or by there being a copper castle with walls and towers between him and the object of his wishes. That inserted "of course" speaks wonders. When he finally sees the princess she really does look so lovely that he simply cannot resist kissing her, for "he was a soldier all over."

Probably only adults take in the subtlety of these details or understand the perspective in the brief comment that one of the *old* ladies-in-waiting was told to sit up after the first night adventure "to see if it was a real dream or something quite different." Do children notice that it is the king and queen, the old lady-in-waiting, and all the officers who sally forth in the morning to see where the princess has been? That was not kind to the army!

"The Traveling Companion" is also one of the first retellings. This is a story about a good-hearted young man who has lost his mother and is soon to lose his father, and who wanders into the wide, wide world. The good John prevents a pair of wicked creditors from throwing a dead man out of his coffin by paying the dead man's debt with the whole of his inheritance. Farther on his journey he is hailed by a stranger who proposes they travel together, and they soon become great friends. The stranger is able to perform strange arts, and these arts are of help to John when he wishes to propose to the beautiful but wicked princess. She has been bewitched by an evil ogre in the mountains; but the traveling companion gets the better of both of them, and helps his friend John to free the princess from the magic spell so that honest John wins both her and the whole kingdom. When the traveling companion has completed his deeds he disappears without a trace—he was, in fact, the dead man, now a ghost, paying his debt to his rescuer for the goodness shown him.

This story is written specifically for children, as is made clear by the somewhat sentimental compassion that the narrator shows toward the characters and the occasional use of child's language ("Ugh, how fierce it looked"). The psychology, too, in several places is as simple as in the folktale ("the wicked men," "the good John") and is how children normally accept it. But the description of the settings certainly exceeds the narrow framework of the folktale. The description of the ogre's palace in the mountain is a wealth of original and imaginative details—and there is great charm about the presentation of the ogre's courtiers who "were so grand and genteel; though anyone with eyes in his head soon saw what they were. They were nothing but broomsticks with cabbages for heads that the ogre had bewitched into life and dressed in embroidered robes. But it didn't make any difference for they were only for show"—An amusing aside about the demands court life makes on people.

Moreover, several of the situations possess such animation that they become familiar and real. The wicked princess causes her old father such sorrows that he can scarcely eat, "and anyhow the ginger-nuts were too hard for him." The king had once and for all said that he would never have anything whatever to do with her suitors, yet he is so full of concern when the new suitor presents himself that he "began to cry so hard that he dropped both scepter and orb on the floor and had to wipe away his tears with his dressing gown. . . . Poor old king!"

Indeed, even the ogre in his mountain responds in a reasonable manner, at least, it is reasonable from his own special viewpoint. When the wicked princess tells him that while she was flying out to the mountain she was whipped so terribly by the hailstorm, he replies, "Yes, one can have too much of a good thing"—a quite natural response for, after all, an ogre is a form of inverted human for whom the most vile of weathers would be the most pleasant.

VI *Beyond the Retellings*

The retelling of old tales was, however, only a starting point for Andersen. With his imagination he could invent in the same style and had at his fingertips the requirements of the genre and the possibilities of the settings.

Folklore figures from legends and tales were often little more than names; but Andersen endowed them with individual features and thus gave them fresh life. A suitable example is found in "The Hill of the Elves." In the Danish woods, where the soil is moist and mists rise up of an evening and sway back and forth like grey dancing shapes, the peasants for ages had felt the presence of all sorts of nature-beings. First and foremost among those were the elf people, who could be dangerous to meet if you happened to pass by when their hill opened of an evening. Andersen was fully aware of this belief and created from it an imaginative humoresque which he himself called "A Firework-Display."

Now, one evening the lizards are scuttling about Elf Hill discussing why so much rumbling and numbling is going on inside the hill. An earthworm lets it be known that distinguished visitors are expected and that a great celebration is going to be held. These distinguished visitors are the Dovre Troll, the largest and most famous troll in Norway, and his two sons, who are looking for wives. The elf girls were already rehearsing their dances outside the open hill and in the middle of the Elf Hill the great hall had been smartened up: ". . . the floor had been washed with moonlight and the walls rubbed down with witches' lard until they shone like tulip petals with the light behind them. The kitchen was crammed with frogs on spits, snakeskins filled with little children's fingers, and salads of toadstool spawn, moist mouse-noses, and cow parsley, beer brewed by the marsh-woman, sparkling saltpeter wine from the burial vault—all most substantial: rusty nails and stained glass from church windows made up the sweets." The Norwegian troll arrives with his two ill-mannered sons, and the feast begins. The Elf King's seven daughters are presented and the troll from Dovre himself takes one for a wife (for he is a widower), while his sons ignore the offered brides, preferring instead to run around blowing out the will-o'-the-wisps who had kindly come to make a torchlight procession. Finally, daylight approaches and the Hill has to be closed to keep out the sun; whereupon the lizards and the earthworm make their final comments on the events.

This is a fantastic party in the realm of the supernatural, and yet it is described in such human terms that the reader practically feels at home. Although Andersen has introduced the whole gamut of the denizens of folklore, as well as the animals of the forest, the happenings at the Elf king's court closely resemble those of an ordinary family: an old respectable housekeeper; daughters to be married off; and bickering over who is to be invited to the banquet. The Elf king only puts in an appearance on the most ceremonious of occasions and, when the guests arrive, is anxious to be seen wearing his gold crown—polished with finest slate-pencil—while standing in the moonlight. The old grey-bearded troll from Dovre is a picture of an elderly Norwegian gentleman, jovial and open; while his two cocksure sons have much in common with another type of Norwegian who in Andersen's day was attracting some rather unflattering attention. The Death-horse is so sensitive that the toe-spinning dance of the Elf girls makes him giddy, and he is compelled to leave the table. Those inquisitive creatures, the lizard and earthworm, are not unlike humans, since the most interesting thing for them is to observe and discuss the goings-on of fashionable people. They look down on each other and distrust each other with typical human pettiness.

VII *"The Snow Queen"*

Andersen was also able to create new fairy-tale worlds without the help of tradition by using his own imagination. "The Snow Queen" is an example of what he could achieve when his imagination was at its most creative. It is also one of his longest tales written during his highly productive period in the 1840s. The main characters are two children, Kay and Gerda, who live in a small town next door to each other and play happily together, until little Kay is taken away one winter's day by the sinister, ice-cold Snow Queen. The Snow Queen is winter, snow and coldheartedness in one person, and she has taken Kay to her kingdom near the North Pole. The story tells how little Gerda all alone searches for her lost play friend and how on her journey to the North comes to the strangest places: to a fairy-tale kingdom where a pair of crows unsuccessfully try to help her in her search; to a castle of robbers; to a Lapp woman and then to a Finnish woman and finally to the ice-encrusted palace of the Snow Queen where she finds Kay who, with an ice-cold heart, no longer recognizes his play friend. She cries on his breast, and her tears thaw and release him so that he can remember things once more. The two children then return to the old grandmother at home.

This story contains a wealth of fantastic and grotesque details. Yet, no matter how strange the conditions are in the places that Gerda visits, the persons still possess something recognizably human about them. The two crows are crows to their very feathertips, almost to their speech, yet at the same time they are good-natured philistines, limited yet helpful, whose ambition is to be employed at court. The robber castle is full of cracks from top to bottom, a large fire is burning on the stone floor of the huge, grimy hall, and the robbers sing and dance while the old robber hag turns somersaults. They readily slaughter people and take pleasure in eating them; the old robber hag prepares to taste the plump little girl who has just been caught, but the old hag's own little daughter takes care of Gerda in her own rough way and promises her that the others will not kill her, "even if I do get angry with you; then I shall do it myself!" When the robber girl draws Gerda down with her to bed she has a long knife in her hand. "I always sleep with a knife," she says, "You never know what may happen." When she is displeased with her mother she bites her in the ear, and her morning greetings to her is, "Good morning, my own darling nanny goat!" Yet the bloodthirsty old hag is not entirely inhuman for, when the morning's work is done and the menfolk are away, she takes a pull or two at a big bottle before having a little nap. Even the unsentimental robber girl, after hearing about Gerda's lost playmate, becomes thoughtful and is moved by Gerda's lasting love for him. The old Lapp woman is also moved by Gerda and writes a few words for her to take to the Finnish woman; the words are written on a piece of dried cod for she has no paper. At the Finnish woman's house they have to knock on the chimney as there is no door. Inside the house everything is just as strange. But the old woman is also human; when she knows the lines by heart she pops the dried fish into the stockpot, "for it was quite eatable and she never wasted anything." Sweat pours down the Finnish woman as she strains to read the strange writing on the magic parchment that will give Gerda the necessary information about Kay. Finally, the Snow Queen's palace is a horrifying fantasy of snow, frost, and cutting winds, and when the gale drops, the reader is frozen to the bone by the deathly silence. Despite everything, the Snow Queen has human charm, thus making it possible for the reader to understand why little Kay likes her.

Is there a basic idea behind this story? Perhaps Andersen thought of it as a description of the innocent child-mind that, like faith, can move mountains, or, in genuine romantic fashion, of cold reason and warm feelings.[14] Kay engages in intellectual exercises in the Snow Queen's palace: Gerda rescues him with her warm love. Somewhere along his way the author seems to lose interest in his idea in favor of the jumble of events, and so too does the reader. This inspired combination of mad fantasy and psychological truth has made "The Snow Queen" immortal.

VIII *"The Nightingale" and Other Tales*

Much the same can be said about "The Nightingale." A summary of events is as follows: The omnipotent emperor of China reads that in a far distant corner of his imperial garden there is to be found a remarkable bird called a nightingale that sings more beautifully than any other bird. She is brought to the court where she enchants everybody with her songs. Her popularity is boundless until the day the emperor receives from the emperor of Japan a mechanical nightingale, a clockwork musical box that can only sing one song but that also glitters with gold and jewels. What an interesting and valuable plaything! How beautiful it is—much prettier than the modest real nightingale which, by the way, has never really felt comfortable at the formal court. Thus, during the fuss surrounding the new arrival, the real nightingale quietly slips off to her freedom in the woods. Indignation spreads through the court when her flight is discovered, but everyone feel consoled with the artificial bird, which is obliged to sing its song again and again until one day it breaks down. It is repaired after a fashion but must only be used once a year.

Soon after the emperor falls seriously ill and is close to death. In the final scene of the tale he lies deserted by everybody, for they believe him dead. He is haunted with memories of his deeds, both good and evil. As faces, they look down upon him, some gentle, some hideous—and among the latter sits Death, gazing at the emperor with hollow eyes. There is no relief for his despair; the artificial bird by his bedside is silent, for there is no one to wind it up. All at once he hears the little live nightingale singing for him outside, close to his open window. She sings all the evil visions away, even death, and, in the morning when his servants come in to see their dead emperor, he stands restored to health before them.

The tale deals with truth and falsehood, with spontaneity and formality, while the setting and events seem just as remote as in "The Snow Queen." With convincing elegance Andersen presents us with a China composed of all the West's shallow misconceptions of the Celestial Empire: a sort of marionette-theater China where everything is of porcelain, gold, or silk, with people nodding their heads like dolls; where conventions are so ingeniously devised as to seem actually Chinese; where the emperor can have his courtiers punched in the stomach after supper when they have displeased him; where those in authority are ridiculously impressed with their own dignity and the common people foolishly ape their masters.

Nevertheless, throughout the whole story a thread of credibility is spun out of the characters who, despite their grotesque Chinese appearance, are people the reader can recognize without difficulty: arrogant courtiers, subordinate commoners, pedantic scholars who are all little worse than their real life counterparts. Absolute monarchy, with the emperor at the top, is depicted quite realistically, with a slight exaggeration that makes things stand out clearer. The presentation of the real nightingale, a symbol of spontaneity and the most warmly human of all the characters, introduces an incomprehensible and disturbing element into a society where formality is the only thing that keeps people alive.

The narrative fully reflects the author's sympathetic yet critical temperament. Wonderful poetry fills the description of the nightingale's wood while stirring pathos pervades the scene of the emperor's deathbed; yet the merciless revealing of human weakness continues with terrifying elegance, often with apparent innocence. While the emperor is lying on his deathbed "the whole country was filled with such deep sorrow, for when it came to it they were all quite fond of their emperor." Is it likely that their sorrow is genuine when described in such a light manner? Most revealing of all is the irony behind the emperor's greeting at the end of the tale: "The servants came in to look after their dead emperor. Yes, there they stood, and the emperor said, 'Good morning!' "

Seriousness and irony, realism and imagination are interwoven in "The Nightingale" to a miraculous unity. Andersen's muse must have watched with great favor throughout those few hours in 1843 during which the story was written from one evening to the following day.[15]

A delicate balance between realism and flights of fantasy is one of the secrets of the tales Andersen either retold or invented within the traditions of folklore. A few tales contain material from sources other than folktales but still possess fairy-tale characteristics. "The Naughty Boy" is based on a short poem by Anacreon, as Andersen openly admitted. The story is about little thoughtless Cupid who one rainy evening is let into the home of a kind-hearted old poet. He feels sorry for the little naked, shivering child, gives him wine and apples, and warms his cold feet. Think! The little boy thanks the kind old poet by shooting an arrow clean through his heart! Naughty Cupid! A few ironic warnings to all readers then follow; they must keep a lookout because Cupid is up to his tricks everywhere and causing harm wherever he goes.

An old Spanish cautionary tale that Andersen happened upon was turned by his imagination into "The Emperor's New Clothes," a story about a vain emperor who is so tremendously fond of fine new clothes that he takes no interest in anything else. One day two swindlers come to the city and offer to weave him a suit of clothes that has the peculiarity of being invisible to anyone who is not fitted for his post or

who is hopelessly stupid. Within the world of the fairy tale there is
nothing unreasonable in this idea: the swindlers exploit it and receive
a large sum of money from the credulous emperor. They weave on
empty looms but nobody, not even the emperor, dares admit that he
can see nothing. Finally, the swindlers declare the clothes to be
ready, the emperor puts them on, and walks in procession through
the city streets. Everybody is taken in except a little child who uses
his eyes and shouts out, "But he hasn't got anything on!" The people
begin to giggle, but the emperor has to maintain the illusion and
continue, procession and all.

The chief idea behind this tale concerns the weakness of people:
they are afraid of the opinion of other people, afraid to see things as
they are, and dare not be honest to themselves. Much truth about
people can be revealed through the apparently innocent fairy tale.

IX   *Stories About Living Creatures*

A second group of tales, realistic in their fashion, uses as their main
characters not people but animals, flowers, toys, and other objects.
The range of such characters is well known from classical fables, a
literary genre long exploited, and one in which La Fontaine had
shown great and original talent. Andersen, however, was to use the
ideas in quite his own fashion. Classical fables are moral stories
demonstrating human weaknesses and teaching the reader about life
and how it should properly be lived. In a few instances pots, pans, and
other objects appear, but otherwise the gallery of characters consists
of a few recurring animal figures who appear side by side without
consideration of zoological probabilities and without the habits the
animals would have in real life. Externally they have adopted human
patterns and behave accordingly.

Andersen's animal world is quite different; there are none of the
traditional lions, asses, wolves, and so on; instead there are only those
creatures that he knew from everyday life. They are always found in
surroundings that fit their natural behavior. Their speech is not
consistent human speech as in the fables, but varies from one type of
animal to another and is marked by the zoological characteristics of
that animal.

Of even greater importance is the fact that the point of view of the
narrative is not necessarily the same as that of a person's. At the
beginning of "The Dung-Beetle" [16] we hear that the emperor had
once been in danger of his life; he had put spurs to his horse, jumped

clean over the fallen horse of the enemy, and thus saved his life. But
the wording of the narrative makes it seem that the horse had taken
the initiative and the emperor had just allowed himself to be rescued.
Here lies the secret: the horse is the main character while people are
secondary. And this is the case in all of Andersen's tales employing
animals, flowers, or objects: events are seen from their point of view,
and we are shown the world as it must appear to them and not to a
human observer. The characters live their own lives, so to speak,
independent of people and of people's view of the world.

How, for example, does the world appear to a mother duck and her
ducklings? Read the famous "The Ugly Duckling" and find out! The
story begins in the country by a manor house surrounded by a moat,
and beneath the huge dock leaves by the water a duck is sitting on her
nest. When her ducklings eventually hatch they stare about in surprise. "Oh, how big the world is!" they say, for, after all, they were
used to lying in an egg. "Do you suppose this is the whole world!" says
their mother. "Why, it goes a long way past the other side of the
garden, right into the parson's paddock; but I've never been as far as
that." At last the big ugly duckling tumbles out of his egg and the
whole new duckling family has to be introduced to the duckyard
where they are to live. Here the ducklings have to learn to defend
themselves, keep an eye open for the cat, and mind that the girl (they
do not know who she is, nor do they care) who feeds the poultry does
not kick them. They have to turn their toes out, not in, to show they
are well-bred ducklings, and they must bow to the duck that has
Spanish blood in her, for she is a duck of the highest distinction in
their small community. The characters think and reason with concepts natural for their surroundings. The little newcomers are judged
according to what a duck should be able to do. That the ugly grey
duckling can swim is a good sign, for then it is not a complete failure.

The ducks' universe is not much more than their yard, the moat,
and the dock leaves; the parson's paddock being the end of the world.
Therefore, it is a great step for the ugly duckling to take when he flees
out into the wide world: he had been teased and chivied about so
much because of his ugliness that he can take it no longer. After a
number of adventures he comes to a little broken-down cottage
where an old woman lives with her cat and her hen. Though this is
another community it is just as circumscribed as the duckyard was.
The inmates know only their home and do not care a fig about the
outside world. Here the duckling has to counter such questions as,
Can you lay eggs? Can you purr and give out sparks like the cat when

his fur is stroked the wrong way? If not, then he has to hold his tongue. Then the duckling remembers that it is lovely to swim in the water and to dive, while to the hen this is a ridiculous idea. Such a thought could never enter the heads of the three inhabitants of the house.

So the duckling once more goes on his way, suffers greatly from the cold winter, but in springtime he finds himself in a big garden with a winding stream not unlike his birthplace. Here he meets three beautiful swans, creatures he had seen once before and admired. But when he sees his reflection in the clear stream he discovers that he himself is a swan. "It doesn't matter being born in a duckyard, when you have only lain in a swan's egg" is the point of the story.

The animal characters differ just as human ones do. The good-natured duck on her nest is of a different temperament to that of the old duck who is paying a call and who always has her experiences and advice at hand and will be offended when they are not heeded. But it is the hen and duck problems that give rise to squabbles and discussion: How long should you wait for the last egg? Can you make good in the duckyard? Who should have the eel's head that has been thrown to the creatures in the yard?

The fate of the ugly duckling is clearly symbolic of Andersen's own climb *per aspera ad astra*, but the immortality of the tale comes rather from the surprising pictures of life seen from the point of view of ducks, hens, and other dumb animals; not forgetting the startling vision of human existence as reflected through the lives of the animals.

"The Happy Family" is also set out in the country, this time in the old neglected garden of a manor house where the burdocks have spread everywhere. In this forest of burdocks live two large old white snails of the type that formerly were stewed into a fricassee and served to fine folk in the manor house. These two snails are the main characters of the story; humans do not appear. The reader discovers how this elderly couple adopt a little common snail as their own, and later on learns of their efforts to find a suitable wife for him. They succeed, hold a lovely wedding, and the old snails express their wish that the young couple might one day enjoy the honor of being taken up to the manor house and being boiled, laid on a silver dish, and served. This wish is never fulfilled, but the family lives on happily in its burdock forest.

In this tale the reader sees and experiences only what snails might see and experience. They know the burdock forest and the creatures that inhabit it: the cockchafer, the earthworm, the ants, and a few others. What lies beyond their little world is not known to them, apart from the manor house where they have heard that the finest snails were boiled and laid on a silver dish. But perhaps the manor house has fallen into ruins and everybody has died, since nothing has been heard from them. That the venerable couple regard themselves as the center of the world and believe that the burdock forest was planted for them and their family is quite reasonable as is the idea that the manor house was there so they could be laid on a silver dish. It is also quite natural that the snail with its shell should be regarded as something finer than the black slug without a shell, and that the slow pace of the young snail bride pleases her future in-laws, for it clearly shows that she is one of the right sort of snail.

Ducks think differently than hens, and again these think differently than snails, for they each have their own backgrounds. So, too, do the characters in "The Dung-Beetle," a tale that has already been referred to. The self-satisfied, somewhat irritable dung-beetle has its home in the emperor's stable but is offended that he does not get golden shoes when the emperor's horse does, so he sets off out into the world where he encounters various other animals and undergoes a number of experiences, pleasant and unpleasant; such as having to lie in wet linen while the rain pours down; being caught by two little boys and tied up in an old wooden shoe that they launch on a lake (of course, the beetle thinks it is the ocean), but fortunately he is rescued by a young girl and eventually returns to the place from which he had started.

He is pleased and satisfied to be back in the stable because for the beetle this is the center of the world while the rest was the fringe of civilization. Only in spots like the stable can things be decent. A hotbed or a dungheap was all right, but to lie in wet linen was terrible, since cleanliness was the worst he could be exposed to. However, the characters that the beetle encounters on his wanderings do not know the stable. They, too, are limited in their concepts of the world but limited in their own ways. The ladybirds enjoy the beauty and scent of the roses and lavender in the flower garden. The caterpillar is preoccupied with the thought that it will fall asleep, die, and wake up as a butterfly. The frogs praise their country for all the glorious rain and dampness; while the most beautifully egocentric figure is the fly that visits the beetle when he is lashed to the shoe. "Delightful weather we're having," said the fly. "This is just the place for me to take a rest and bask in the sun. You've found a cosy spot." "What nonsense you're talking! Can't you see that I'm tied up?" "I'm not tied up," answered the fly and promptly flew away.

X   Stories About Inanimate Objects

For the tales about objects the same analysis is valid as for those about animals. A typical example is the tale "The Shirt Collar." There are no human beings in it except that at the beginning we are told about the collar being the property of a swell gentleman, but after the first sentence this person disappears and thereafter everything is seen from the collar's point of view. The tale is realistic in the sense that nothing occurs that, given the opportunity, we would not notice for ourselves. The collar comes into the wash with a garter, is dried in the sun, ironed, is frayed at the edges, is trimmed by the big scissors, receives a violent jag so that he has to be thrown away, and is sent to the paper mill together with other rags to be changed into white paper.

These trivial events take on quite another perspective when seen through the collar's eyes; that the collar and the garter touch in the washtub signifies proposal and rejection, contact with the iron and scissors indicate the same. The big pair of scissors with her long legs could only have been a great ballerina, and when the collar was given too big a cut it was not due to clumsiness on the part of the user of the scissors (for the collar knew nothing about such a person) but due instead to the scissors being indignant at the importunity of the collar, and the meeting with all the rags in a bag at the paper mill is turned into an opportunity for the collar to boast to the rags about all his love affairs. Thus the material events are given a personal justification; the persons are rational individuals, not inanimate objects.

At the conclusion of the tale we are returned to the human beings by an ironic admonition addressed to the reader: Consider, the collar was turned into "this very bit of white paper we have before us, on which the story has been printed. It was all because he boasted so terribly of what had never actually happened. So let us remember not to behave like that; for, after all, we might find ourselves one day in the ragbag and be turned into white paper and have the whole story of our life, even the most intimate details, printed on the front, so that we ourselves have to publish it abroad, just like the collar."

This playful aside at the end of the tale grows naturally out of the narration but can not be regarded as a moral, the truth of which would have had to have been demonstrated by the events. In the actual story the shirt collar lives his own independent life with his carefree proposals and his cheeky boasting. The tale draws an amusingly critical portrait of a certain type of person.

Most of the tales about objects are realistic along the lines of "The Shirt Collar." "The Shepherdess and the Chimney Sweep," for example, is set in a sitting room, and the characters are objects usually found there: an old cupboard with a figure of a grinning satyrlike person carved on it; a large Chinaman in porcelain who could nod; and on the table beneath the looking glass a shepherdess and a chimney sweep who, too, were both made of porcelain and equally brittle and so naturally suited to become engaged.

Between these figures the drama takes place. The wooden figure, ever since the cupboard had been placed in the room, has remained staring at the table under the looking glass—a fact that could only mean that he had alarming intentions toward the sweet little shepherdess. The old Chinaman who, naturally, was made of china claimed, though he could not prove it, that he was her grandfather, and he had nodded his consent to the suitor who would make a good match, for he was sure to be made of mahogany, and had a cupboard full of silver. The shepherdess is in despair and begs her chimney sweep to flee with her out into the wide world. They climb up through the chimney, a way he ought to know, and get right up to the top where, alas, the world seems far too big to the little fragile lady and despite every argument of the chimney sweep they return to the security of the room they had left. But when they get back they find the Chinaman lying in the middle of the floor in pieces, by chance as we humans would probably say, but in reality because he had tried to chase after the runaway couple. The couple are seized with remorse: it is their fault that grandfather is broken; will it be expensive to rivet him? Fortunately, the family have him repaired, and the loving couple look pleadingly over at the old grandfather to stop him from giving her away to the distinguished suitor; and he follows their wishes because, well, now a rivet prevents him from nodding consent to the satyr. So the loving couple stay happily together until they at last get broken.

Here it is apparent that the world of these characters is just as limited as that in "The Shirt Collar." They only know the living room and each other—they do not know who owns the house and the objects. It is only in passing that mention is made of "the children who lived there" and "the family." Also in this tale the material events are given personal justification, for the characters are living, thinking beings. Only the two little porcelain figures exceed their material possibilities, yet even so they maintain their china doll characters so faithfully that it is easy to forget that their expedition to the top of the chimney conflicts with their natures.

In this context mention must be made of that remarkable tale "The Story of the Year," even if it stands a little apart. It is a description of the seasons and their changes but, as in the above tales, they are described from an unexpected viewpoint. It starts as a realistic picture of everyday life. There is deep snow and it is bitterly cold. In the little town as much snow as possible has been pushed aside, and in the cleared passages people meet and pick their way past each other as best they can. Evening comes and the uppermost layer of snow turns crisp and hard in the frost, so hard that it easily carries the sparrows which hop about talking of the weather and the New Year—and immediately the sparrows have become the main characters. The people in the streets vanish from the horizon and we find ourselves in quite another world. From now on we hear the sparrows' chatter, and we follow them when soon after they fly into the open nature, out to the winter-covered fields. Shivering they hop about in the snow; they meet an old raven who lives there and who therefore knows that the strange old man down on the snow drifts is Winter himself. And as time passes, the characters change, and nature changes appearance with them. Winter leaves, and the laughing children of spring make their entrance, grow up and become Summer and his spouse; but when autumn comes they both leave for the south and are replaced by the King of the Year, who finally sits bent, waiting for young Spring while the Christmas angel is going through the land.

The tremendous events of nature have passed in front of the reader—but the humans stay away. The comments on the events are given by the birds, not by the humans. Apart from the opening scene humans and human conditions are only mentioned in passing. The sun scorches the cottage wall but we do not hear more about it, not even who owns the cottage. When the thunder storms of summer approach, people in carriages, on horseback, and walking hurry to come under shelter; but who they all are, where they belong, where they are going, and what becomes of them later is of no interest. Summer's entrance is what we are to hear about, and the scurrying people are only included to complete the picture. Even the familiar church bells at Christmastide are only mentioned because they are the birthday chimes for nature's new ruling couple who are soon to come. The humans are quite outside the events of nature and do not come into contact at all with the living forces of nature and the beings that move around out in nature. It is not the numbed peasant but the birds who see and recognize the heavy figure of Winter sitting on his snowdrift on the hill—and the little old woman looking out into the first spring sunshine, and thinking how wonderful everything is, does not see nor does she speak with the two spring children who bring all the blessings with them. If we hear anything about humans at all, it is through the comments of characters in nature, and they all see humans from the outside. One of the town sparrows mentions that it is living with a human family who has been so sensible as to set up some nests for birds, and give them a little to eat; but it can only guess what the intention can be—presumably it is just so that the humans can have the pleasure of seeing them, otherwise they would not have done it. The humans behave foolishly in a number of ways; they set off fireworks on New Year's Eve, as is the custom in Denmark, relates a tiny, frozen sparrow, and are quite wild with joy that the year is over, even though the New Year if anything is worse than the old. The humans have made an error in calculating the date, and instead of reckoning New Year from when spring arrives, they have made a calendar that just does not fit with nature. Summer's serious wife also shakes her head at the humans; when the most beautiful late-summer has come they plough the fields again! More and more is what the humans want to gain, she says.

Humans have been placed outside the events, and that is the secret of the story. Nature's characters are in the center of the story. The humans are only included when they take part in the events of nature or when the sparrows come into contact with them. The external surroundings are the same as those we humans know and live in; they are just seen and understood from another side.

XI   *The Human Elements in the Fairy Tale Characters*

Animals and objects have lives of their own, independent of people, yet nevertheless each life is intensely human. The explanation lies in that they think and feel as people but within the limitations imposed upon them by their zoological and material nature and by the environment in which they exist. Thereby each of them is a portrait, miniature in size, and extraordinarily well drawn. Andersen's tales are full of people in disguise, sometimes seen in a passing glimpse, other times in greater detail.

Some of the characters reveal a clearly defined full-size human type with many nuances. The snails in "The Happy Family" are self-satisfied, good-natured, staid representatives of a philistine class; the dung-beetle is a somewhat irritable rounded specimen of self-importance; the shirt collar is a superficial boaster ceaselessly trying to present himself as more than he is.

The fir tree in the tale of that name is the ambitious yet always unsatisfied soul: when it is a little tree in the wood it is in a passionate hurry to grow, and when it has grown it longs to go out into the world like those trees it had seen felled and taken away. It takes no pleasure from what is going on at the moment but is always longing for what is to come. Eventually it is cut down and sold as a Christmas tree. It is then placed in a living room and decorated, and experiences the family's Christmas while all the time trembling with excitement at the thought of what will happen next. Now, though, its prime has been reached and there is no more pleasure in store. After the festivities it is put up into the attic and here it begins to understand that now its life is behind it and that it has been so busy thinking about the future that it had not seen the pleasures lying right in front of it. Next spring it is thrown out into the yard and chopped up for firewood, " 'All over!' said the poor tree, 'if only I had been happy while I could! All over!' "

A contrast to this melancholy story is "The Flax" where the main character is an always satisfied optimist. It can be plucked from its wonderful open spot in the field, bruised and broken, made into linen, cut and pricked, torn into rags, made into paper and used for writing on—yet its comment on all these painful ups and downs is simply, "You can't always have it so good!" It is thankful for the honor and advancement shown it, even to the final great honor of being burned and changing into sparks that fly directly into the sun.

Love as it might shape up for the average person is described in several tales. In "The Shepherdess and the Chimney Sweep" it is obstructed young love, while in "The Top and the Ball," sometimes called "Sweethearts," it is unrequited love that fades with the years; the top falls in love with the ball and feels that they can fittingly become engaged for they do live together in the same drawer, and he can spin and dance and she can bounce. But she fancies herself to be too fine for such a match. The next day when the little boy is playing with the ball she bounces so high that she never comes back. The top sighs and longs for her, and the years pass until "it became nothing more than an old love affair." Suddenly one day the top is painted gold all over so he looks very handsome and he whirls and dances. But then he, too, jumps too high and lands in the dustbin: but who else is lying there among all the rubbish? None other than the distinguished ball of old that certainly had come to look woefully shabby. "I have been lying up in the wet gutter," she tells him, "and it has been rather a trial, you know!" But the top is careful not to say a word, and is presently found and removed from the dustbin and returned to the other toys in the house, but he never speaks again of his old love, for it is "bound to fade away when your sweetheart has spent five years growing sodden in a gutter; you can't be expected to know her again if you meet her in a dustbin."

"The Butterfly" is another tale about love and engagement yet seen in a different light: the butterfly wants a sweetheart among the flowers, but which one should he choose? There are far too many to choose from and, besides, there is something wrong with them all; the violets are too romantic, the daffodils too bourgeois, the lime blossoms have such a lot of relations, the sweet pea withers too quickly, and so on. At last he proposes to the mint. But he is rejected because she thinks they are both too old to marry, "Friendship, but nothing more!" So the butterfly remains a bachelor and as it happens is caught and set on a pin in a box (by whom it is not said), "Well, here I am on a stalk like the flowers. . . . I expect it's like being married; you're certainly pinned down then!" And the thought consoled him.

The multitude of varied portraits gain their clarity and distinctness from the simplification that is possible when human nature is expressed through this special sort of character. An additional refinement lies in the humorous tension existing between the characters' nonhuman environment and their only too-human thoughts and feelings. The reader is permitted to see his own and other people's weaknesses from a new viewpoint.

XII   Short Stories and Situation Pictures

A similar element of surprise does not exist in those sketches and short stories in which the main characters are people. Nevertheless, many have the touch of genius. The best known is "The Little Match Girl," written in 1845. The editor of a periodical had sent three illustrations to Andersen with the request that he write a story for whichever one he preferred.[17] Having chosen the picture of a girl selling matches in the street, Andersen proceeded to tell the story of a little girl who is selling matches on New Year's Eve. She shivers for it is terribly cold and she is poorly dressed. She had been wearing her mother's great big slippers but had lost them when two carts came whizzing past and she had had to scurry across the road. She walks around barefooted but nobody will buy matches from her. She does not dare go home without having sold anything because her father would beat her, and besides, it is also cold at home in the miserable attic where she lives. She huddles in a corner between two houses and strikes a match to warm herself on, and then another and another, and in each flame she sees a new sight: a warm stove, a beautifully laid table with a roast goose which she knows everybody eats on New Year's Eve, a lovely Christmas tree with shining candles, and finally her dead Grannie who had always been kind to her, and who takes her into her arms and carries her up to God. The following morning people find the little girl sitting in a corner frozen to death with a bunch of spent matches in her hand. " 'She was trying to get warm,' people said. 'Nobody knew what lovely things she had seen and in what glory she had gone with her old Grannie to the happiness of the New Year.' "

No sentimental phrases mar this story that is remarkable for its soberness; there are only factual elements: the street mishap; the misery of her home; the hallucinations provoked by exhaustion; her death. At the end of the story no commiseration is expressed; we are simply told what the people thought at the sight of the dead girl, and how they were wrong.

A less famous story that deserves to be better known is the little pearl entitled "Heartbreak." The first part of the story takes place in a manor house in which the narrator meets a good-hearted, middle-aged widow who has called on the owner of the house on a business matter. She is accompanied by her pug dog; and both characters are brought vividly to life with just a few words. About the pampered pet Andersen simply writes, "Pug nose and porky were his looks." In part 2 of the story the scene has moved to the market town where the widow lives. The pug is dead, and the widow's grandchildren are putting the final touches to its grave in the backyard. It is a splendid grave, and all the children from the street are allowed to see it for the price of a trouser button. They all cheerfully pay because in their small world all events are of importance, even those which seem to adults to be insignificant. Moreover, the pug's grave is a sensation, so those who do not see it will be missing a great treat—and what is worse will be left outside the group of friends. Such a fate befalls a little ragged girl who does not own a button. She has to remain outside the gate and watch the others go in. When they have all seen the grave and have gone away, she sits down and bursts into tears:

"she alone had not seen the dog's grave. That was heartbreak, as bitter as an adult's can often be."

With brilliant understanding Andersen has recreated the child's world of experiences in a most compact story. He recalls how it was to live in such a small world and how it felt to be left outside. He also remembers what it was like to be poor, and he did not forget that his mother's drudgery had forced her to seek comfort in the bottle. These memories, together with other experiences from the hard life of the poor, formed material for "She Was No Good," a tragic story about the daily labors of poor folk. "She Was No Good" can be seen as a forerunner of the social writings that were to come at the end of the nineteenth century.

The other short stories and sketches have not contributed greatly to Andersen's world-wide fame. Nevertheless, even in these more conventional stories there are amusing characters, both comic and pathetic, such as the affected general in "The Porter's Son," a monstrosity of ridiculous class arrogance and snobbishness, or the outspoken and unsentimental noble woman Marie Grubbe in "Hen Grethe's Family." Short pointed portraits were always Andersen's forte.

XIII   Narrative Art [18]

No matter which category of tale Andersen is telling the style is completely his own. Part of its originality lies in the reader's constant awareness of the narrator's presence in the middle of the listening audience. He narrates and explains, claims his audience's attention, even exchanges words with them, and along with them enjoys the story he is telling. At times he speaks as if he was a man who had experienced everything himself and perhaps even knows about the real facts of the matter and the innermost thoughts of the characters; at other times he argues with his audience as to how the phenomena in the narrative are to be understood.

The unquenchable vivacity of the style is also due to Andersen's living intensely in the situations and events he is describing. At the beginning of "The Ugly Duckling" the whole description exudes the warmth of the pleasure he derived from the summer: "It was so lovely in the country! It was summer!" At the very moment of narrating he seems to see and experience that wonderful landscape.

There is even more: he assimilates to his characters and makes their thoughts his own. They slip imperceptibly into the narration as indirect speech or *style indirect libre* (i.e., the account reflects the wording of the person in question). When the soldier in "The Tinderbox" is at the bottom of the tree recovering the tinderbox for the witch and the money for himself, he has to go into three rooms, each of which contains a dog sitting on the money, each dog being larger than the one before. In the third room, so the witch had told him, the dog has eyes as big as the Round Tower in Copenhagen. When he gets there, "Oh, but it was horrible! The dog in there really did have eyes as big as the Round Tower" (the soldier's thoughts). When our brave soldier has spent all of his money and has to live in a tiny attic room, "none of his friends ever came to see him for there were so many stairs to climb" (his friends' explanation). Then when he was rich again and had changed back to fine rooms "all his friends remembered him again at once and were tremendously fond of him" (friends' words to soldier).

In part one of "Heartbreak" the good widow puts her pug dog down and he "began growling. After all, he had gone with her for enjoyment and the sake of his health and so they had no right to put him on the floor" (the pug dog's thoughts).

Occasionally the narrative moves without warning from the thoughts of one character to those of the next. When the nightingale has won favor with the emperor of China by her singing Andersen writes, "Now she was to remain at court and have her own cage, with leave to go out for two walks in the daytime and one at night. Twelve attendants were to accompany her, each holding tightly to a silk ribbon fastened to her leg. There was absolutely no fun in a walk like that." The word "leave" shows that this is the court's view of the matter, while the last sentence must be the nightingale's opinion.

Not only the thoughts and feelings of the individual characters are brought out but also those of the people who are attending or might be attending the events. In "The Top and the Ball," when the top has jumped too high and disappeared, we are told: "They looked and looked, even down in the basement, but he was not to be found. Wherever had he got to?" This question is obviously posed by the searcher, but it might equally well be asked by any person present, even the reader of the tale. After the artificial nightingale has been repaired, though alas not very satisfactorily, the learned master of music "made a little speech full of the most difficult words, declaring that the bird was just as good as ever—and so of course it was just as good as ever." To whom is it just as good as ever? This must be the courtiers and the whole foolish mass of blindly obedient people, all those who heard the master of music's declaration. "The Nightingale" ends with the emperor, having survived the crisis of his illness, rising in the morning to greet his servants who are coming "to attend their dead emperor. Yes, there they stood, and the emperor exclaims, 'Good morning!' " That outburst, "Yes, there they stood," could clearly come quite naturally from anybody witnessing this grotesque scene, including, of course, the principal character, the emperor. Actually, it could also come naturally from the narrator and his readers.

There are, in fact, many instances where it is just not possible to differentiate between the thoughts and feelings of the principal characters, those of other characters present, and those of the narrator. They all blend into one living consistent picture. On the dung-beetle's wanderings in the world he is caught in a rain storm and looks for shelter; he catches sight of something white; it was some linen laid out to bleach. "He came up to it and crept into a fold of the soaking fabric"—this is the narrator's objective information—"Of course, this could not be compared with lying in the warm dung in the stable"—here we have slipped over to the beetle's point of view—"but there was nothing better to be had here"—this could well be expressing the beetle's dissatisfaction with his lodging place, but could also be the narrator's objective comment—"so he stayed where he was for a whole day and night, and the rain stayed too"—once more we are back with the narrator's observations.

Like this, life sways backward and forward in the narrative. The narrator stays in the background or steps forward depending on the circumstances. But the continuity of the narration is never broken. Even the author's reasoning asides grow organically from the situation as, for example, at the conclusion of "The Shirt Collar" or "The Naughty Boy."

The mastery with which Andersen controls this sensitive suggestive style is clearly shown in the great philosophical fairy tale "The Bell." At the close of day, in the narrow streets of the city—begins the tale—people often hear a strange sound like the ringing of a distant church bell. The sound seems to come from the depths of the mysterious wood, and people are curious and ask each other what it might be. Eventually, some people do go looking for it, but they soon grow tired, give up their search, and make do with a pleasant day in the woods. One of them claims, however, that he has found an explanation, incidentally not a very convincing one. He is rewarded with the appointment of Universal Bell Ringer, and every year he writes a little essay on the strange phenomenon. One Confirmation Sunday the boys and girls who have just been confirmed have a desire to find the unknown bell; three of them, however, are prevented by some reason or other from joining in the search. The rest depart but do not go far enough. All but one stop off on the way, the one who continues is a prince. He makes his way through the wild wood and finally just before sunset climbs upon some rocks, from which place he can see stretching before him the ocean rolling its long waves in toward the shore. While he is standing caught in the beauty of the evening, one of the three who had been prevented from joining the search comes toward him from another path. This poor boy has had to return the confirmation clothes that he had borrowed. They take each other by the hand and there in the midst of magnificent nature they hear right above their heads the great invisible bell of nature and poetry and become one with the universal spiritual forces that give life to nature.

This story stands a little apart from the other fairy tales because the mysterious bell is not something tangible: it is an abstract symbol of the romantic experience of nature as a spiritual force. Nevertheless, the narrative radiates human nature. The writer is present in every line, he lives in the situations and characters, his sensitive temperament is there in the immense pathos as well as in the subtle irony. There is imposing strength and beauty in the final picture of sea and sunset with the prince and the poor boy watching from the high rocks. The ecstatic mood possesses extra strength when contrasted with the description of city life at the beginning of the tale. There can be no doubt as to Andersen's attitude toward the inhabitants, young and old, of the city, but his criticism rarely comes to the surface. One or two insignificant expressions give rise to a suspicion that the citizens' search for the mysterious bell is not so very serious: they are only out to enjoy themselves. Of the ostentatiously appointed Universal Bell Ringer there is the laconic remark that every year he wrote a little essay, "but no one was any wiser than before." Then there is the confirmation! "The parson had spoken with a fine sincerity"—and then in four lines comes the respectable nonsense said on such occasions. The eloquence of the account is such that the reader can actually see everybody nodding approval at the parson's words while being borne along by the sentiments. Andersen holds back his skepticism for the empty phrases and only records what is said. The explanations of the three children as to why they cannot join the search are expressed in such differentiated language that three different voices can be made out. The first one is from a girl for whom a ball-dress was at least as important as the sacred occasion: she "had to go home to try on her ball-dress, for it was on account of this dress and this ball that she had been confirmed this time, otherwise she would not have come." The second is "a poor boy who had borrowed his confirmation suit and shoes from the landlord's son, and he had to return them not a minute later than he had promised." The third one "said that he never went to strange places without his parents and that having always been a good boy he would go on being one, even after being confirmed. And that's not a thing to jeer at," adds the narrator to the unsuspecting reader—and then observes, "—but that's just what they all did." Reality is harsher than people's good intentions.

Andersen was able to switch from narrative to general reflections, from gravity to fun, from poetry to commonplace triviality with an adroitness and elegance that no other Danish writer has been able to approach. His command of his mother tongue was perfect. He knew precisely how colored a word to use in a lyrical or pathetic description, and he was familiar with all the secrets of those small adverbs that abound in the Danish language and hint at the speaker's opinion or reveal his mood. Andersen understood where to place them in ambush; with a single word or two he could bring a character alive or unveil it in all its meanness.

Andersen's narrative style contains many secrets, but only some can be discovered. The Chinese master of music in "The Nightingale" wrote twenty-five volumes full of the most difficult Chinese words to explain the mechanism of the artificial bird. This was not possible with the real nightingale.

XIV Idea Tales

Andersen was not a philosopher; he was unable to present a complete world picture or a consistent view of life. He was a creative writer, not a thinker; in other words, his immediate feelings toward life's phenomena were more powerful than his deliberations about them. But still—sometimes it did happen, mostly in works produced after 1850, that a tale was constructed around a general idea or a didactic thesis that was to be demonstrated through the course of events. This is true of "The Red Shoes," for example, which tells about a poor little girl who loses her parents and then is taken into a fine, wealthy home. She is given good clothes and a pair of fine red shoes and she is so taken up with them that she cannot think of anything else, not even at her confirmation in the church. Her vanity takes the upper hand, she disregards the old lady, her benefactor, who is ill and dying, and goes to a ball with the red shoes. But then her punishment falls. A strange old soldier (we are not told who he is) bewitches the shoes so that they dance off with her; she cannot control them nor can she get them off. Night and day she dances off until finally, in desperation, she begs the executioner to cut her feet off. But even that does not stop her vanity; she wants to show herself in the church but has to turn back because she sees the red shoes dancing in front of her. Finally, she humbles herself and goes into service at a vicarage. She does not dare to go to church, but one Sunday when the hymns waft over to her, her heart breaks and she finds peace in death.

It is rare for an Andersen tale to be so clearly moralizing. In practically all of his other tales the interest is in the events, which are unfolding freely with their own inherent logic. An admonition or two sometimes closes the story, but they have no influence on the action. In "The Red Shoes" things are different. All events, including the supernatural, appear to be directed to showing the reprehensible vanity of the girl and the misery it brings with it. There is no inner coherence in the events beyond that required by the moral demonstration. Naturally it is a personal matter whether you regard the events as reasonably coherent. But to the present writer the events in "The Red Shoes" lack cohesion and justification. For example, who is the old soldier? Is he the Devil (as one modern critic believes)? [19] Or is he a representative of Providence who is to bring the girl back from her delusion? Why does his face appear above the treetops in the forest at night?

A comparison with the tale "The Buckwheat" is illuminating. In this tale a thunderstorm moves across a cornfield; all the corn bends before the storm; only the buckwheat holds its head stiff and therefore is singed by lightning (as can, in fact, happen). Its unbending arrogance has been punished, as is said at the end. But this concluding moral observation does not determine the events, for the storm crosses the landscape as it needs must do by nature, and with natural consequences. The moral is only the writer's reflection afterward. In "The Red Shoes" the moral idea is demonstrated throughout the story. The explanation of this display of moral zeal, so unusual in Andersen's works, is presumably that he is judging himself. In part the story rests on a recollection from his own confirmation. [20] For the solemn occasion he had been given new boots, but with dismay and remorse he realized that he was more taken up with them than with the religious ceremony. He never forgot this episode.

Of course, Andersen was absorbed in the problems of his time, particularly those that an artist had to face: his position in the bourgeois society and the contrast between genuine art and the lack of understanding of it shown by the public at large. Andersen wrote about this in "The Swineherd," "The Nightingale," and "The Goblin at the Grocer's," among others, but always in such a manner that the events had their own independent life.

A more fundamental problem that engaged him throughout his life was this: Why do some people have a happy existence while others undeservedly have to suffer sorrow and misery? His solution was that given to him by his childhood Christianity: the account had to be squared in another life. "The fairy tale has its harmonic dissolution here on earth; reality most often places it beyond this life into time and eternity," is how he expressed it in "The Thorny Path of Honor"; but he also gave this idea an artistic form several times after 1850, particularly in the two long tales "A Story from the Dunes" and "The Philosophers' Stone," both written in 1859.

The former tale belongs to the group of realistic short stories, and begins in warm Spain where a young newlywed couple, wealthy and happy, are talking about the eternal life that was promised mankind. The young man is of the opinion that it is arrogant to demand a life after this one, when in the present life one receives so much good. "Yes, *we* receive it," says his wife, "but think of all those who suffer in this world! Were there not a life after this one, then everything on this earth would be unfairly shared out." Thus the problem is presented, and the fate of the young couple confirms its seriousness. He is sent as the Spanish ambassador to Russia. His ship crosses the North Sea but in a terrible storm is wrecked on the west coast of Jutland; there are no survivors save the young wife, who in a humble fisherman's hut gives birth to a son; but she dies immediately afterward. The baby is adopted by childless fisherfolk, and then follows an animated description of the toilsome yet, in a way, happy life in the stern dune landscape of west Jutland, where sand flies in the wind and in storms can migrate far into the country.

The dark-eyed southern boy becomes a fisherman and sailor like the other people on the west coast. He travels far, once even to Spain, to the very town where his parents had lived before their unfortunate journey—an ironic twist of fate of the sort that romantic writers were prone to use. The effect is strengthened when the poor ship's boy one day on land sits down to rest for a while outside a dignified palace, but is driven away by the porter—the boy has no idea that this is the very palace where his unknown grandfather lives old and alone.

When the boy has grown up, his troubles and sufferings begin: first an unhappy love affair, then an unjustified accusation of murder, which puts him into prison. A year passes before he is declared innocent and released. Better times come for the much tried young man. A merchant from Skagen, the town at the northernmost point of Jutland, takes him into service as a fisherman. It is a good home; he falls in love with the pretty daughter of the house, and she with him, all seems well. But things were to change. When Jørgen, as he is called, fetches her back from a visit to Norway, the ship springs a leak and sinks off the coast of Skagen. He attempts to swim to shore with her, and they are picked up by a fishing boat, but the young girl is dead and he has suffered irreparable brain damage when he struck his head against the anchor of a wreck protruding out of the water. For some years the wretched fellow sits lifelessly around, remembering nothing, feeling nothing. "Only hard times, pain, and disappointment were his lot. . . . The All-loving God had to and would give him compensation in the other life for what here he suffered and lacked"—this is Andersen's comment on the fate of his hero at this point in the narrative. Jørgen ends his life by leaving home one stormy evening and, his mind clouded, walking into the church of Old Skagen; the gale blows up the sand as never before, it drifts up high around the church, blocking the entrance. Nobody can get into the church the next day—and nobody knows that the young man lies there as in a gigantic sarcophagus.

The story shows, according to Andersen, that God will never fail but will bring life's account to order, if not before then in eternity. Of course, a story cannot prove the truth of a belief (as one English critic wrote about *To Be, or Not to Be?* which was based on the same idea), and "A Story from the Dunes" should be regarded as one of Andersen's energetic attempts to convince himself of the validity of a faith in eternity. But the theme has inspired him to a lively and precise description of the specific milieu in the poor districts of Jutland.

The second tale from 1859, "The Philosophers' Stone," is a strange and grotesque religious fantasy based on the concept of Christian faith. In the East lives the wisest man in the world, who knows everything except what happens to a man's soul when he dies. In his

"Book of Truth" he can read about what has happened, what is happening, and what will happen, but on the page where the truth about life after death is written the writing is so faint that he cannot read it. But the wise man knows that out in the wide world live the three fundamental ideals: the Good, the True, and the Beautiful. These three hold the world together and from the pressures that they sustain a precious stone is produced, and this is the philosophers' stone. It contains the answer to the mystery of the world (whether this is the answer to the question about death is not clear in the story). In order to find this precious stone the wise man's four sons set out into the world, one after another, but fall foul of the Devil's schemes; they tire of their search and remain in foreign countries. Finally, the wise man's fifth child, a young blind girl, sets out to fetch the stone and bring back news of her brothers. Whereever she journeys she spreads warmth and love; she gathers every grain of Truth, Goodness, and Beauty, and in her closed hand they turn into a single glittering jewel. She returns home with her brothers, and when she opens her hand the jewel shines on the white page of the "Book of Truth" that should tell about the certainty of a life after death; and there is one word: Faith. The wise man has the answer to his apprehensive question.

The story can justly be called an idea-tale, for it should show that the soul, when confronted with the problem of death, will find peace in the Christian belief in another life—a serious subject but presented with both gravity and wit. The introduction to the story is a hilarious discourse, and in the course of the story there are passages with the most unexpected bizarrely humorous ideas. The cheerful passages do not, however, weaken in any way the pathos of the conclusion. That Andersen could hold deep gravity and wild gaiety together in an artistic whole is proof of his supreme control of his mode of expression.

On the other hand, in "The Most Wonderful Rose in the World" the deep pathos is carried through from beginning to end: the almighty queen, who loves roses, lies ill and can only be saved from death if she is brought the most wonderful rose in the world, the one that is an expression of the highest and purest love. People come from near and far with the most beautiful roses they have, but it turns out that it has to be a rose of another, intangible sort: the rose of science, the red rose on the cheek of a child or on the cheek of a young girl when, in purity and love, she receives the altar sacraments, or the white on the cheek of a mother when she fears for her ailing child. But none of these is the right one. Then her little son enters and reads from the Bible about He who allowed himself to be crucified in order to save mankind. "Greater love cannot be found." And the queen receives new life from the rose that rises from the pages of the holy book—the most wonderful rose in the world.

The Christian message of love and salvation is the unifying idea, but it is expressed through the fairy-tale form; that is to say, the events take place in a milieu of the same sort as those in the folktales that Andersen rewrote. There is a wise man, a queen, and a court, and a people for whom the queen's well-being is a personal affair. Even more important, the boundary between the tangible and the abstract or spiritual phenomena has been erased. They are not kept apart. They stand on equal footing. Reality and symbol are interwoven. The roses lying on the coffin of Romeo and Juliet change within one sentence to something intangible: the poetry that has grown out from the tragic fate of the famous pair of lovers. In what follows the roses are something concrete yet at the same time something more. In the course of the tale this flower becomes laden with experiences and feelings until the climax: the queen sees the rose rise from the pages of the Bible and thereby experiences the great message of salvation, perhaps even (although it is not stated) an assurance of eternal life.

XV   *The Message Behind the Fairy Tales* [21]

Few of Andersen's tales are built around a clearly defined idea. Nevertheless, the tales as a whole do express a universal wisdom of life. In the multiplicity of events in his tales Andersen has put down thoughts about mankind, the world, and life in general, thoughts that have grown out of the extensive experiences and adventures of his own life.

First, Andersen makes no bones about which kind of person is worthy of respect and which is not. Those who accept the gifts life offers with gratitude are always depicted with sympathy. The person with a warm heart or the one who throws himself into life with a cheerful spirit and pays no heed to formalities will eventually defeat the scheming rationalist. The loving Gerda rescues her friend Kay from the Snow Queen's palace of cold intellect; the cheerful, singing nightingale is stronger than Death at the emperor's bedside; Simple Simon (in the tale with the same title) wins the princess. On the other hand, the self-satisfied philistine who is only interested in his own affairs and nothing more, who arrogantly judges all and sundry from his own limited experience, and who is always willing to strut in borrowed plumage (like the Beetle and the Shirt Collar), is mercilessly exposed in the fairy tales to laughter, whether directly or indirectly does not matter, for the intention is always plain. The narrowmindedness of the philistine was an abomination to Andersen.

Second, the fairy tales contain quite precise ideas about the universe and the evaluation of its phenomena. These are far from always being explicitly expressed. Yet it is striking that no form of common universe exists for the characters of the tales. Each group of creatures lives within its own surroundings which for the individuals of that group is *the world*: they are unaware of what lies beyond. Nor is there any uniform opinion about existence concerning what is better or worse. Just as great a difference exists among the humans. The little girl with the matches has few thoughts in common with the princess on the pea; children and adults live in separate worlds.

Even the same surroundings and the same events can look fundamentally different. In the great fairy story set in Switzerland, "The Ice Maiden," the characters appear on three levels: (1) the Ice Maiden and the other sinister spirits of nature who rule the great icy wastes of the glaciers, for whom humans are ridiculous insignificant creatures who in their arrogance believe that they can control the forces of nature; (2) Rudy, the young chamois hunter, his sweetheart, and their families; and (3) the domestic animals which, so to speak, see the humans from a lower level and who, by the way, think that humans are strange, illogical creations. Time upon time these three completely different views of life come into conflict; the most charming occasion being brought out in the little scene where the kitchen cat relates what it has heard the rats say about happiness. Happiness to them was to eat tallow candles and to have their bellies filled with putrified pork; while Rudy and his sweetheart had said that the greatest of happinesses was understanding each other. "Whom should we believe, the rats or the sweethearts?" is the cat's question.

The answer to this reasonable question must be that both are right, in their own ways, since the appearance of the world and its objects depends on the eyes that are doing the looking, and we humans, who are often mutually in disagreement, have no grounds on which we can claim that our view of the world is the only correct one. In the fairy tales there are countless other creatures that have other opinions and whose words have as much weight as those of the humans. This point can be seen at the conclusion of "The Marsh King's Daughter" which, like "The Ice Maiden," also contains three levels: the trolls, the humans, and finally the stork family; the storks watch and comment on the events from their point of view. While it is the fate of the human characters that makes up the main theme of the tale, it is the storks' comments that conclude the story. The final words in "Heartbreak," a tale described earlier, state directly that what might seem unimportant to adults might be of extreme importance to children. When the pea pod in "Five Peas from one Pod" gradually turns yellow, the five peas that are inside say that the whole world is turning yellow, "and they had a perfect right to say so," adds the narrator. Different beings must inevitably have different thoughts and opinions about the world, and they have a right to have them, the small and insignificant just as much as the great. When judgment is passed in the fairy tales it is only passed on those who believe they have a monopoly of the truth: they are handled roughly.

Now to the third point: What thoughts about life as a whole are to be found in the fairy tales? Is life good or evil, just or unjust? Has it anything to offer us pitiful humans, or should we turn our backs on it?

At a first glance the tales provide self-contradictory answers to these questions. Andersen's works can both affirm the highest of expectations and shatter all illusions. Comfort can be found, for instance, in "The Traveling Companion" and "The Wild Swans," where the pious and good principal characters go through much hardship but nevertheless are finally happy—and, naturally, in "The Ugly Duckling," an inspired symbol of Andersen's own life where the most important moods, events, and, in part, characters from his strange career have been recast in other dimensions and thereby made universal in an impressive hymn of praise to life. Many of the other fairy tales contain similar reassuring thoughts: everything will take up its rightful place, the good will not be forgotten, arrogance and wickedness will suffer defeat, and, if not at once, it is because the Lord has time to wait.

But far more fairy tales depict quite a different course of events. Nearly all the short stories are about people for whom things have gone badly in life and who finally are left with their frustrated hopes, alone and disappointed—if, that is, they do not find freedom and reconciliation in death.

The bitter pessimism revealed here lay deep in Andersen's mind and is also to be felt in some of the shorter fairy tales, though nowhere so movingly as in "The Story of a Mother." One cold winter's night Death fetches a little, sick child, and the desperate mother runs out into the darkness to overtake him. She meets Night, comes to a crossroads where there is a thorn bush all frosted over, and then reaches a lake that she must cross; at each place she has to sacrifice something of herself in order to find out which way she has to go. When she finally gets to Death's great greenhouse, Death has not yet arrived and when he does he cannot, and will not, surrender the child.

A harrowing story, a monument to mother-love as well as to the mercilessness of existence. In form it is a fairy tale; mythological beings such as Death appear; natural phenomena, Night, the Thorn Bush, the Lake, are personified; the mother's sorrow makes her travel even faster than Death, for in the world of the fairy tale the soul is stronger than the body. But "The Story of a Mother" is far from being a folktale. The subject is handled with supreme imagination and brilliant mastery. We are also far from the noncommittal pleasure of "The Tinderbox" or the elegant irony in "The Shirt Collar" or the optimism of "The Ugly Duckling." "The Story of a Mother" speaks with relentless earnestness; Night, Thornbush, Lake, and Death, all show a heartrending remorselessness toward the poor mother. For all her sacrifices she gains nothing save an awareness that perhaps it would be even worse for the child to be brought back to life. Without a strong faith in the Providence of God the reader of this terrifying story will be horror-stricken by the meaninglessness of life.

Matters are no better in "The Shadow," [22] which tells of a learned man whose shadow leaves him and, after a number of years, returns for a visit. The shadow has blackmailed his way to great riches and now has the desire to go to a health resort, mainly because his beard will not grow and something must be done about it. Will the learned man go with him? Well, things had been going badly for the scholar, and the shadow is willing to pay his expenses on the simple condition that they exchange roles: that the learned man should recognize the shadow as a person and act as his shadow. He hesitantly accepts. At the spa the man and his shadow meet a princess who is taking the waters to cure her disturbingly oversharp sight.

She falls in love with the elegant, prosperous shadow who, to all appearances, is a person, and who moreover explains to her that the gentleman accompanying him is his dressed-up shadow. The shadow and the princess become engaged, and when the learned man, who is scandalized at the engagement, tries to disclose the shadow's identity he is thrown into prison and put to death. The wedding then takes place.

There are a few fairy-tale features in the story. The shadow liberates himself from his master and begins his own existence; that it is possible to have a disturbing disease of being able to see too well is quite natural; and that a rich, eccentric gentleman dresses up his shadow as a person is no more out of the ordinary than taking the waters in order to get his beard to grow. But these points are only markers along the way in a shocking drama about a respectable, well-meaning, study-bound scholar who becomes the powerless slave of his own shadow, his former servant and companion who, without disdaining any means no matter how low, climbs up the social ladder to achieve his ambition. The two characters are painfully true to life; the same can be said of the princess who, although she is clever, is not clever enough to see through a swindler, even though he is but a shadow she could very nearly see right through, as it is said with deadly irony about her when her amorous glance rested upon him. The bitter philosophy of the tale is that there are wise people who want to do good, but their wisdom and goodness do not help them—and there are ruthless people who do just what they want and emerge victorious. There are no redeeming features. "Such is the world and like this it will always be," says the shadow.

For those people afraid of the pitilessness of existence and the infamy of mankind there is no comfort to be found in this macabre tale.

But even though existence, in the fairy tales as well as in reality, can be brutal and unjust, and sorrows more frequent than pleasures, the reader is left in no doubt that life is worth living. One must take things as they come. Sorrows are heavy, but if we accept them as part of the pattern of life they can also bring us blessings (as shown in "The Last Pearl"). Everything depends on oneself. With open eyes and receptive mind it is possible to discover that existence is rich and beautiful, full of events, both big and small; that the world contains a multitude of people and other beings, each with his own individuality, all so different that we need never be bored if we will just look and listen. For the hearse driver in "A Good Temper" life is a great and cheerful theater, and when the young copying clerk in "The Goloshes of Fortune" and the young aspiring poet in "Something to Write About" have their eyes and ears opened stories buzz about them. All the flowers in "The Snow Queen" tell their stories to little Gerda, who has an open mind.

It is possible to experience something interesting or enjoyable from even the smallest of things, anything that people do not usually

find interesting. An old, discarded street lamp becomes the joy of the
watchman's family in their little living room in the cellar; a pea flower
invokes the will and the courage to live in a young sick girl in the attic;
and a ray of sunshine can be a sermon about the gospel of life.
Situations where nothing particular happens can contain both beauty
and poetry for those who can see and hear. However, it is not
everybody who can. The little fir tree in the fairy tale of the same
name is so preoccupied with growing up and being big that it has no
time for the sunshine, and the fresh air, or for its many fellow trees
both pine and fir, or for the village children chattering so gaily
together while they gather berries. But, come to that, the fir tree
never understood how to live.

XVI *Challenge To The Modern Reader*

The fairy tales emphasize the gospel of an open mind and immediate emotion; they speak the case for the small, overlooked creatures,
and they let it be understood that existence is richer and greater than
our limiting notions of good and evil, so rich as never to be exhausted.

It is plain that such a philosophy has spoken to many hearts and
given much comfort to many people. It will also appeal to modern
readers. But by reading the tales carefully and by drawing conclu-
sions from what is told, the reader will be more disquieted than
comforted. Even the portraits of the philistines are enough to fright-
en the reader: Was it not only in those days that people were like that,
or are there many of that type today? Are you yourself so narrow-
minded? Do you dress up in borrowed plumage like so many of the
philistines in the fairy tales? Do fine phrases also pour from our lips?
Are we slaves of catchwords, slogans, and other simplifications of
reality?

A chill runs down your spine when you see the gulf separating the
characters, including the human ones, in the tales. Are people really
so different? Can we not somehow become homogeneous? Are not
our democratic ideals valid? Are those not due to one-eyed idealists'
rejection of an inescapable reality? The fairy tales are one great
rejection of any uniformalization of life and any comformalization of
people. Was Andersen, as a writer, more realistic than we are?

Furthermore, is the great physical universe that we are brought up
to believe in, the ultimate truth? Is it possible that things are not dead
and that natural forces are not impersonal? Our knowledge of physics
says one thing while the artist in Andersen claims another. Should we

believe the physicist or the artist? The fairy tales say that if you live intensely with your immediate surroundings they will come to life for you, and then the great mechanism loses all interest. Does the modern reader accept such a viewpoint?

Finally, the fairy-tales' message about the riches of life: Do we understand how to accept its gifts both large and small? Are we just as open as the writer and many of his characters? Or do we go through life deaf and blind, unable to respond to the little experiences that it has to offer us? Do we have a superficial and rash relationship to our surroundings?

The fairy-tales are not a harmless and innocent reading. If you know how to read, they leave your soul disturbed. Andersen's worldly wisdom, his knowledge of people and life was far beyond the normal man's.

XVII   *The Explanation of his Success*

Andersen was a mediocre dramatist, an average poet, a good novelist, and a brilliant travel writer. But in the fairy tales he attained perfection. That it was precisely this form that suited his genius was due to an exceptional conjunction of external and internal circumstances: a special social background, a special temperament, and a special artistic talent.

The social background was his childhood in poverty in Odense. As far back as he could remember he had known legends and tales, and, what was of even greater importance, he was completely familiar with the world that was the setting of these folktales. Up to his fourteenth year he had lived among people who were unaffected by the physical view of nature that the cultured class had been brought up on. For the peasant class there was nothing unreasonable or absurd in what the tales contained. Nor was there for Andersen. A feeling for the mystery of existence was part of his makeup. Other Danish writers had composed or retold tales, but they only knew the world of the fairy tale from literature. Andersen knew it from his own experience and was able to give his narration quite another authority, a far greater credibility than his fellow writers could. His roots among the common people were a social handicap at the beginning of his career but proved in the fullness of time to be his fortune as an artist.

Andersen's psychical constitution was the second prerequisite for the writing of the tales. For a start, his ungovernable imagination made the fairy tale form more natural for him than the novel or the play. In these last two genres attention has to be paid to the practical likelihood of events. But in the fairy tale so much can happen that the improbable can become probable; true, there ought to be a certain logic behind the events, but there is far greater room for imagination.

Moreover, Andersen was born with a sensitiveness which meant that he experienced his surroundings with a far greater intensity than most people. He was, so to speak, caught up in what he saw and was able to forget himself in the phenomena of the surrounding world. Animals of all sizes became thinking, reasoning individuals to him; even so-called inanimate objects received a personality. He wrote to Ingemann in 1843, "I have ample material [for the fairy tales], more than for any other form of writing: often it is as if every fence, every little flower said, 'Look at me a little, then you shall understand my story!' And if I do, then I get the story!" [23] It is quite natural that animals, flowers, or toys in his fairy tales are living personalities, for that is how he experienced them in real life. When Andersen created, his observations of nature were married with human experiences and the results were characters that were animals, objects, etc., with human reactions. The Dung-beetle is a dung-beetle on the surface and a human beneath.

Of equal importance was the enormous range of his psyche. He had maintained the child's spontaneity in his reactions and its intimacy with its surroundings, while at the same time he had an adult's matter-of-fact reflection. It was this ambivalence of mind that enabled him to write for both children and adults at the same time. He was able to be on a child's terms with a tin soldier while depicting experiences that could enrich every adult.

Finally, there is the third prerequisite: his special form of artistic talent, or if you like, its limits. Andersen's difficulties lay in holding on to a large-sized composition or a detailed and varied characterization. His strength was the brief glimpse of a person, the elegant phrase, the rapidly outlined situation. The fairy tale was as if created for his episodic gifts. The genre did not permit circumstantiality, and at the same time it was so free that Andersen was able to locate his countless fragmentary observations about nature and people practically anywhere, either as a small portrait of a type or as a personal aside. He could freely jump from the animal kingdom to the world of humans, from narrating for children to reasoning for adults, from gravity to lightheartedness and back again.

Thus the fairy tale became the most direct way for him to express his expansive and capricious temperament. Here in a poetic sense he felt at home, and this perhaps explains the strange fact that here he was so inordinately painstaking with the form. The fortuitousness and negligence that often mark his poetry and his plays are never present in the fairy tales. On a number of occasions he had rewritten his plays in response to criticism from the theater's literary advisers; but no one was a better judge of how a fairy tale should be written than himself. He polished his language and gave free reign to his imagination. There is strict moderation and clear consistency in the supernatural events. Just how unrelenting he was can be seen from the extant first draft of "The Shepherdess and the Chimney Sweep" where his imagination flowered beyond all bounds. With an unerring instinct he toned down the tale until it was perfect.[24] No precipitate passage was allowed to pass. No fairy tale was sent to the printer until Andersen was convinced that it could not be improved. Depth of experience and clarity in expression are the hallmarks of his fairy tales.

CHAPTER 4

Criticism, Influence, Research

I *Popularity and Criticism*

A. Denmark

FROM the very start Andersen's fairy tales were popular among the Danish reading public. Although the first reviews were often unappreciative, Andersen rarely had reason to be dissatisfied with professional criticism. In the main the reviews of his fairy tales throughout the years were friendly, but from a modern viewpoint are not particularly profound. The words imaginative, childish, and naive appear in practically all of them, even in those about the volume containing "The Shadow." As late as 1852 a reviewer of the tales published in that year said that they sprung from childish thoughts, were to be understood childishly, and that the reader's heart, like the author's, ought to be childish and sentient.[1] One of Andersen's fellow writers, Henrik Hertz, who was a lyrical poet, an author of comedies, and a poetical theoretician, did not go much deeper, for he considered the tales to possess humor, a cheerful atmosphere, and a satire that was both amusing and entertaining, as he wrote to Andersen in 1845.[2]

A profound evaluation of Andersen's fairy tales first appeared in two long reviews published in 1855 and 1863.[3] The first review characterized Andersen as "an imaginative, sensitive, impressionable, clear-sighted, gifted personality with a sharp instinct and a strong faith"; the reviewer mentions Andersen's evocative powers, his understanding of the poor and lowly, the little people of everyday life, and the beauty (or the poetry as one said in those days) of their lives. The reviewer discussed the philosophy expressed in the fairy tales, and formulated it in a couple of lines that Andersen himself regarded as exceedingly pertinent: "The fairy tales pass a cheerful Judgment Day upon appearance and reality, on the external shell and the internal kernel. A dual current flows within them. An ironical surface current that plays and jokes with all and sundry, playing shuttlecock with great and small; and then the deep undercurrent of seriousness that justly and truly puts 'all in its rightful place.' This is the true and Christian humor."

The second reviewer, in 1863, took up other questions. He drew attention to the fact that the fairy tales in the course of time had changed character, for the tales written prior to 1850 had shown that fusion of thought and form characteristic of classic poetics: a philosophy of life, if you will, had thus found immediate expression in fairy-tale form. The tales written after 1850, however, rarely show this absolute unity and completeness; instead, they present a living, realistic conception of the surrounding world and a deeper psychological understanding.

Finally, in 1869, appeared Georg Brandes's fascinating essay,[4] the most comprehensive that had been written about Andersen's fairy tales. Andersen was exceedingly pleased with this essay, which, with its many fresh observations, was like a joyful excursion through the fairy tales. Brandes draws attention to the fact that by telling stories for children the narrator can get down to the most elementary experiences of everybody, and by so doing can reach a world-wide audience. About the art of writing in spoken language, Brandes says, "When writing for a child you must try to melt the changing intonation, the sudden breaks, the descriptive hand movements, the fear-provoking air, the sudden change to a coming smile, the jest, the caresses, and the appeal that awakens the drooping attention—to melt all this into the rendering; and as he cannot literally sing, paint or dance the event for the child, so you must conjure the song, painting and air into your prose so that it lies in it like bound forces that rise as soon as the book is opened." Brandes investigates the Spanish source of Andersen's "The Emperor's New Clothes" and states that Andersen had brilliantly simplified the story and given it a new inner cohesion. Furthermore, he mentions the idyllic properties of the subjects and settings; no gigantic human problems, no menacing eroticism; no wild nature, for the tales are filled with domestic animals, not the beasts of the jungle; everything takes place in familiar protected surroundings. According to Brandes, Andersen's strength lay in him being in his soul part child and thus being in harmony both with the nineteenth century's sympathy toward all that was naive and with the Danish national character.

B. Germany and Britain

In Germany the tales were just as popular as in Denmark, and Andersen received much evidence of his popularity on his journeys in that country. A complete picture of the reception that the German critics gave to Andersen's production cannot be given, since no exhaustive investigation has yet been made. However, some impression can be gained by examining the rather random collection of German reviews to be found in the Royal Library in Copenhagen. In these reviews *The Improvisator* and *The two Baronesses* receive virtually unqualified approval, *Lucky Peer* is described as sympathetic entertainment, in *O.T.* and *Only a Fiddler* the descriptions of milieu are praised, while *To Be, or Not to Be* is characterized as a failure. The poems aroused little interest. The travel books and the dramas are kindly mentioned but with great reservations. As far as the fairy tales are concerned, the German reviews emphasize the childlike naiveté, although it was often added that the fairy tales had a deeper meaning that children could not understand. On the whole the reviews are sympathetic, though they contain more critical words than might be expected. Andersen's *idée fixe*, that he was more appreciated in Germany than in Denmark, can scarcely have its origin in the criticism, but more likely in the sympathy shown by the general reading public, and the friendliness and admiration that he encountered privately. Moreover, it would be interesting to know whether he had read the comments made about his memoirs in *Literaturblatt* on 23 June 1849, where the reviewer criticized the long-winded descriptions of his meetings with royalty and important people, and was surprised that Andersen allowed himself to be intoxicated with these distinguished acquaintances and failed to notice that the revolution would soon sweep them all away.

What is known about Andersen's literary fortunes in England is the result of the unflagging research of a Danish scholar, Elias Bredsdorff, who for many years headed the Department of Scandinavian Studies at Cambridge University.[5] Andersen's works were immediately welcomed by the English-reading public. In 1845 Mary Howitt's translations of the first three novels were published, soon to be followed by translations of the fairy tales, which became so popular that no fewer than six different editions came out in 1846. The critics welcomed the novels, particularly *The Improvisator*, while the fairy tales were received with almost unqualified enthusiasm, and they were given more than praise. Several English critics showed a surprising depth of understanding of the peculiar nature of the fairy tales and of their literary value, considerably deeper than that shown by contemporary Danish criticism. Of particular weight was a review in the influential periodical *The Examiner* which drew attention to the fact that in the fairy tales the sea-people, animals, flowers, and so forth each retain an individual personality, and that they all speak and think with this individuality. "They all talk in character." The review added that Andersen understood "the necessity of adhering to verisimilitude," in other words, he always tried for a degree of probability in the events within the tales.

One critic emphasized the elegantly turned satire of man's actions, and several critics were fully aware that the fairy tales were more than just children's stories: that children can enjoy the wonder of the tales but that adults "can see the wisdom enshrined in the fiction." It goes without saying that the critics also discussed whether the stories contained sufficient morality and whether the children would understand that morality.

C. The United States

Andersen never visited America,[6] and contrary to his usual practice, his contact with the American-reading public remained a remote one, and was even late in being established.

That an interest in his works existed in America was brought to his notice as early as 1846 when he met a friend, the famous Norwegian violinist Ole Bull, in Marseille. Bull had just returned from a concert tour of the States and told Andersen that his novels had been published there and that his name was widely known. Of course, Andersen was pleased that he had "crossed the great ocean," as he expressed it.[7] Soon afterward the fairy tales were published there, and his fame in the United States was assured. This fame was evidenced by the fact that Andersen encountered many Americans who knew his name. In 1850 a Dane wrote from New York to say that he was repeatedly being asked whether Andersen might consider undertaking a tour of the United States. Andersen certainly wanted to do so, and for a period in the mid-1850s he was seriously contemplating such an undertaking. One of Andersen's old friends, the Swedish authoress Fredrika Bremer (1801–1865), who had been living in America in 1849–1851, had come to Copenhagen sometime in 1854 in company with her married friends Marcus and Rebecca Spring. Marcus Spring was a New York businessman, philanthropist, and socialist. The couple earnestly requested Andersen to visit the United States, and two years later Spring even offered to arrange the whole trip for him. But nothing came of it, mainly because of Andersen's fear of crossing the Atlantic, a fear greatly increased by the sinking of the *Austria*.

Nevertheless, Andersen's works constantly sold well in America. However, he never received a penny from these American sales, for they were all pirate editions reprinted from the British translations from 1845 onward. In America, as elsewhere, there was no copyright protection for the works of foreign writers. Therefore, for this and other reasons Andersen was fortunate to be contacted by a young gifted American author of children's books, Horace Scudder (b. 1838), the editor of the *Riverside Monthly Magazine for Young People*.

It all started when Scudder sent Andersen an extremely friendly letter and enclosed an enthusiastic review he had published about Andersen's works; the accompanying letter expressed his personal admiration. Both parts pleased Andersen greatly, as can be seen from his diary,[8] but strangely enough he did not reply, nor did he to a couple of subsequent letters; in fact, six years passed before he responded. The patient Scudder had twice invited him to contribute to the *Riverside Magazine*, with the offer of payment. "I fear that while your name is a household word with us, you have not received that just return from publishers which is every writer's due." Only too true! But Scudder and his publishers, Hurd and Houghton, were honorable men, and Andersen was now able to have a proper contract, though on the understanding that Andersen's contributions, because of pirating dangers, "should be sent in advance of their publication in Denmark and Germany, say three months in advance."

Andersen accepted the terms, and a number of Andersen's later tales were published in New York before they were published in Danish. Moreover, much to Andersen's satisfaction, Scudder proposed to arrange the publication of an Author's edition of his collected writings, including *The Story of My Life*, with additional material covering the years 1855–1867. The project got well under way but unfortunately was not a great success with the public and publication had to be halted. The reading public wanted the fairy tales which were readily available in cheap editions; there was little lasting interest in the remainder of his writings.

The contract for the complete writings was extremely favorable to

Andersen who received fees far in excess of what he was accustomed to receive from abroad. This was the first time he had received money from the United States for any of his books, which had been best-sellers there for more than twenty years.

The translations were undertaken by a number of different hands, while the incredibly busy Scudder, who had with time taught himself Danish, always carefully revised them, "endeavoring to give those touches and quaint turns of expression which a long study of your writings has made me acquainted with." [9]

The exchange of letters between the old writer and the young "literary hack," as Scudder called himself, shows just how tactful and amicable a business correspondence can be when it is conducted between two such warm and sensitive people. Through their discussion about fees, deadlines, and so forth it is possible to trace the flowering of a sincere friendship between these two men, who were never to meet.

An additional, and unusual, link with America was formed in the summer of 1874, the year before Andersen's death. He received a clipping from an American paper from which it appeared that there were rumors that the old writer of children's stories was living in straitened circumstances and that grateful American children had started a collection for him. Even worse, though, was the statement, according to the article, that Andersen himself had said that he had never received as much as a single dollar from America.

The ever-apprehensive Andersen was at once terrified: to discover that he was considered to be a pitiful pauper! What would Scudder be thinking after he had loyally undertaken to obtain a decent fee for Andersen! And now this regrettable misunderstanding was traveling around half the newspapers in America! More clippings soon followed, and even an American minister arrived with a small sum of money as a form of advance.

This annoying and ridiculous story led to a number of sleepless nights for Andersen, and his friends found it difficult to lessen his anxiety. The matter had to be settled and the American public told the truth at once. Andersen wrote a letter to the editor of the *Philadelphia Evening Bulletin*, Gibson Peacock, in which he expressed his gratitude for the beautiful thought which had touched him deeply, but he had to inform his American readers that he was not a poverty-stricken writer deserted by his friends and abandoned by his country: "my homeland is not one of those that would permit its creative writers to suffer want." Moreover, though it was true that he received practically no renumeration for the translations of his works, there were occasions when he did, as for example from his American publisher. He concluded his letter with a request to have "my statement brought to the knowledge of your readers."

Peacock printed the letter. In all, Andersen received two hundred dollars from the children's collection plus a sumptious work entitled *Picturesque America*, which is now in the Andersen Museum in Odense. Soon afterward Andersen received an extremely cordial and reassuring letter from Scudder, who had understood the situation immediately. That was the end of the peculiar affair, although there were severe repercussions in Andersen's unstable spirits.

As was the case with German criticism, so too no investigation has been made of the reception that the American critics gave Andersen's works. Hopefully, this task will eventually be completed by an American admirer of Andersen.

D. Translations into English

The British translations of the fairy tales have been the object of a close study by scholars such as Elias Bredsdorff.[10] The Scudder translations have been examined by Erik Dal.[11] The results of these studies have been discouraging. With good reason Andersen was dissatisfied with the early translations. Some translators used the German texts, others tried their best with the original Danish, but their command of the language was not sufficient. They committed a variety of blunders and converted Andersen's elegant Danish into a clumsy English. Later translators did little better. Some attempted to turn Andersen's consciously negligent narrative style into something more formally correct; others expanded the short precise sentences with explanatory additions; while still others incorporated a clear moral or changed the endings of certain tales that seemed too sad; finally, there were many who gave their translations an extra childish tone in the worst possible children's story style. Some of the translators committed several of these crimes at one and the same time. Few translators, apparently, understood the subtle refinement of Andersen's style.

The tendency toward childishness dominated and was responsible for the general literary fate of Andersen's works. The interest in his novels soon died in England and America while the fairy tales lived on but, regrettably, only as reading matter for children. From the beginning perceptive critics had observed that the tales were written just as much for adults, but this perception was drowned under the success that the tales had with children. Of course, it is true that the first tales were called "Fairy tales told for children," but publishers and translators failed to notice that, beginning in 1843, Andersen had removed the "told for children" from the title page, or that he later used the title "Fairy tales and stories," or that a large number of these later stories could only be comprehended by adults. So it came about that the tales were relegated to the nursery, and the translations were made accordingly.

This distortion has continued to the present day with the reprinting of spurious translations and with "adaptations for young people," "stories retold from . . . ," etc.[12] The consequence of this has been that the enormous reading public in the Anglo-Saxon countries does not know Andersen's fairy tales: instead, readers have been supplied with a number of children's stories composed by hack writers who have stolen what they wanted from the Danish author. That the tales when they left Andersen's hands had been distinctive literary master-pieces is something that the reader has no chance of finding out. In fact, people often do not know who he was, and this ignorance is not confined to the Anglo-Saxon countries. For example, the Swiss news-paper *Neue Züricher Zeitung*, which is regarded as one of the best informed newspapers in Europe, described him a few years ago as "the Swedish writer H. C. Andersen."

Fortunately, this century has produced English translations that are faithful to the original. These have been undertaken by people who have rediscovered the literary merits of the fairy tale and have understood the distinctive characteristics of Andersen's language and style. These translators were either Danish by birth (Paul Leyssac and Jean Hersholt) or have taken great pains to master the complex-ities of the Danish language (R. P. Keigwin and Reginald Spink). But even these highly competent translators have been confronted with almost insurmountable problems; first, because the Danish language in itself is extremely sensitive to ironic nuances, and second, because Andersen understood how to exploit these possibilities to the full. Even the best of translators can be forced to expand the text slightly in an attempt to convey these nuances of style and often still fails to present Andersen's version. That less competent souls have been unable to comprehend Andersen's language or at least have failed to reproduce it is not really surprising.[13]

II *Andersen's Influence*

As mentioned above, Andersen's novels, plays, poetry, and travel books are in the main only of secondary importance today. If, however, these works be considered in relation to the literature of his time it will be found that as a novelist Andersen was something of a pioneer. In the early decades of the nineteenth century the novel was an almost ignored genre in Denmark, and Andersen's contributions marked the commencement of a rich development.

His dramatic works could not compete with those of his contemporaries Heiberg and Hertz and did not leave any traces on subsequent Danish drama. Nor could his poetry stand out above that of the other Danish poets of the period; even though a few of his poems are still read, it cannot really be said that his poetry has had any influential role in Danish literary history.

Travel books had been written in Denmark before Andersen's time, for example, Jens Baggesen's *Labyrinthen* (1792–1793), a sentimental journey in Laurence Sterne's style. However, Andersen's form and style were far more modern, and very few of the many Danish travel descriptions published in the last one-and-a-half centuries bear comparison with *A Poet's Bazaar*.

Andersen's influence, of course, depends on the fairy tales and can best be determined by the interest in and knowledge of them in his own time and in our day. In his lifetime his tales were translated into most European languages, and in 1875 as a tribute to the writer on his seventieth birthday, an edition of *The Story of a Mother* was compiled in Copenhagen in fifteen languages: Danish, Swedish, Icelandic, German, Low German, Dutch, English, French, Spanish, modern Greek, Russian, Polish, Czech, Hungarian, and Finnish. The publishers regretted in the preface that a Serbian and a Croat translation arrived too late for press, and they had been unable to obtain information about the translations into Italian, Portuguese and Welsh. Nor had they been able to get hold of the translation into Bengali.[14]

After Andersen's death the number of translations increased steadily. In 1894 in St. Petersburg the same tale was published in twenty-two languages, among them Armenian and Tartarian,[15] while in Copenhagen in 1944 *The Emperor's New Clothes* appeared in twenty-five languages,[16] including Turkish, Arabian, and Chinese. In Japan there has always been an extremely large interest in Andersen's writings, not only the fairy tales; *The Improvisator*, translated at the turn of the century by the Japanese writer Igai, has had a large reading public.

There are now translations of Andersen's tales into more than one hundred languages.[17] Only the Bible has a greater dissemination. A four-volume anthology in Russian (1894–1895) has been the basis of the translation to a large number of the languages spoken within the Soviet Union. The tales also reached Africa. In India *The Story of a Mother* and possibly others were known and treasured in Andersen's lifetime.[18] It may be added that many foreign readers have no knowledge of the author. Andersen's fairy tales have become a genre designation in themselves. They have attained what is probably the highest position that a creative work can reach: an independent existence as a source of energy, as a fountainhead of inspiration for both experience and reflection.

The one-hundred-and-fiftieth anniversary of Andersen's birth was commemorated throughout the world with lectures, theater performances and film shows, radio and television programs, articles in newspapers and magazines, and in some places with drawing and writing competitions in schools. According to information collected by the Danish Foreign Ministry a total of 173 memorial ceremonies, 240 Andersen exhibitions, and 283 soirées were held. Furthermore, there were 1,200 radio broadcasts and several thousand articles. Schools in thirty-five countries commemorated Andersen. New editions of his books came out in twenty languages.[19]

The attendance at these memorial ceremonies throughout the world indicates the exent of Andersen's fame. His tales must have left their print in the minds of people everywhere—to what extent and how cannot, naturally, be measured. An indication may perhaps be gained through the words said to have been spoken by Rabindranath Tagore: "Danish schools actually did not need the Bible or . . . other books for the education of children, for there they have Andersen's tales."

On top of this, the tales have been a source of inspiration for artists of all sorts. The tales have been illustrated innumerable times; and films, plays, ballets, and operas have been created on themes from them, as well as based on Andersen's own life. Finally, thousands of approximate versions have seen the light of day—to the regret of Danes, who would prefer that foreigners know the tales in something like their original masterly form.

Has Andersen had any influence on writing in Denmark? Not really, for to copy him or to continue the genre he created is almost impossible, since his was so closely linked to his own artistic personality. He did not, therefore, create a literary school. It is true that Carl Ewald (1856–1908) wrote fairy tales, but they lack Andersen's sensitive imagination, and contain, in the main, natural history, often in a somewhat didactic presentation. On the novelist Henrik Pontoppidan (1857–1943) the influence was practically negative. One of his major novels is entitled *LykkePer*, but the fate of the hero is diametrically opposite to that of Andersen's protagonist. Pontoppidan's short story "Ørneflugt" ("The flight of the eagle")—about the tame eagle which one day tries to fly out into wild nature as a free bird of prey but which has to return humiliated—concludes with these words: "It's no use to have been hatched from an eagle's egg when you've grown up in a duck yard—" in clear disagreement with the ending of "The Ugly Duckling": "It doesn't matter being born in a duckyard when you have only lain in a swan's egg."

Johannes V. Jensen (1873–1950) admired and loved Andersen's fairy tales and used the same short narrative form in his small, sketchlike lyrical pictures, which he called "Myther." He also wrote an hilarious counterpart to Andersen's "What Father Does Is Always Right" (originally a folktale), which describes a peasant who sets off to market in order to sell his horse or to exchange it for something else. In Andersen's tale, the peasant swaps about several times, each time with a worse result, and finally returns home with a sack of rotten apples. But his sweet wife thinks this is excellent because she knows that father always does the right thing. Jensen, who was born in Jutland, believed that this cheerful lack of business acumen was typical of people coming from Funen, such as Andersen, but that those from Jutland had a better understanding of the art of trading. Jensen therefore wrote a story of the Jutland peasant who sets off with a sack of rotten apples and returns to his surly wife with a horse.

A number of contemporary Danish writers could well have found impulses in Andersen's works, especially Villy Sørensen (b. 1929), who in his fairy-tale-like *Sære Historier* (*Queer Stories*), sometimes used capricious turns of language that might have been learned from Andersen.

Andersen's most important influence on Danish writers, however, consists in his epoch-making break with literary convention in his mode of narration. The bold introduction of spoken language set a definite mark on subsequent Danish prose. After Andersen it became common practise for Danish writers to use the simple and free-expression form of spoken language.

III   *Research on Andersen* [20]

Only some years after Andersen's death—when people were at some distance from his overwhelming personality and remarkable lifework—could the scholarly study of Andersen's writings begin. These studies have focused on two main areas: (1) Andersen's life and personality and (2) his works, particularly his fairy tales.

As mentioned earlier, Andersen's autobiographies are not completely reliable; consequently, a major difficulty faced by scholars has been the uncovering of Andersen's family background and his early days in Copenhagen. Indeed, great efforts have been expended in clarifying precisely how much Andersen withheld, retouched, or rearranged in *Märchen meines Lebens*. Credit for throwing light on these problems belongs to the Danish scholar, H. Topsøe-Jensen, who spent many years checking on the accuracy of Andersen's memoirs. These, together with the collections of letters, have been published by Topsøe-Jensen with extensive commentaries. With the assistance of these publications it is possible to trace Andersen practically day by day throughout most of his life. Through them it is possible to form a multifaceted picture of Andersen's complex personality.

Moreover, this latter point has been the subject of an independent study made by a psychiatrist, the late Professor Hjalmar Helweg, who on the basis of his experiences as a doctor attempted to arrive at a diagnosis of Andersen's state of health, physical as well as psychical. Helweg's study has been fundamental for our understanding of Andersen's psychic constitution.

The study of the fairy tales commenced at the turn of the century. The most important research in this field has been carried out by Hans Brix, Valdemar Vedel, and Paul Rubow. Initially, the focus of inquiry was not the tales themselves; rather, scholars attempted to discover the personal background of the fairy tales, that is, through letters and other biographical documents to trace which personal experiences Andersen made use of in his tales. The reverse procedure was also used; that is, the tales and the novels were analyzed so as to throw light on obscure points in Andersen's life. In short, the research adopted the genetic-biographical methods current in the period.

The influence that past and contemporary literature had had upon him was also investigated so that it became possible to determine just how much of what he wrote was of his own invention. It was easy to ascertain that Andersen in his younger days had read the German romantics, and that he admired Walter Scott; but it was also necessary to find which other authors he imitated.

Finally, the position of the fairy tales in the history of the genre has been investigated. Rubow, in his fundamental study published in 1927, presented a survey of the various genres that, so to speak, are to be encountered in Andersen's fairy tales: fable, fabliau, legend, folktale, romantic art tale. Rubow went on to show how Andersen used these genres in a novel way. Many other points, such as the ideas, form, style, and language of the tales, were discussed in Rubow's work.

In subsequent years research has changed tracks. Even though the term structuralism was not yet in use, at least not in Denmark, its ideas were in the wind. There were good grounds for objecting that the earlier methods drowned the actual works beneath an interest in how the tales came into being, and how they could best be placed in existing categories. According to such critics, it was the literary works themselves that were of prime importance; it was these that ought to be studied, and, if they were to be understood, then they had to be regarded as independent organic entities. As far as Andersen's tales were concerned it was the task of literary research to try to grasp and understand them in their originality, that is to say, to find the way into their innermost characteristics, which give them their entity and their power and make the fairy tales Andersen's and nobody else's.

It was on the basis of such considerations that the author of this present book described the world, or more correctly the worlds, of the genuine fairy tales, not the short stories or the lyrical pictures, and analyzed the inner coherence of the events of the fairy tales.

The religion contained in the tales and thereby Andersen's personal religious beliefs have been the subject of two short studies. However, here the problems are not so great. Andersen was a devout Lutheran and was brought up with the rationalistic Christianity of the eighteenth century, which, as Andersen understood it, declared that there was a benevolent God who looked after everything for the best, and an eternal life awaiting those who by their efforts had deserved it. These simple ideas were held, despite scruples, throughout his life by Andersen, as well as by the majority of his contemporaries. Moreover, it should be added that Andersen felt himself to be particularly under God's protection, practically to the point of expecting that Providence would intervene whenever life's burden was excessively heavy. It was this belief that supported him during his darkest hours.

On the occasion of his one hundred and fiftieth anniversary in 1955, the museum in Odense published a large study entitled *H. C. Andersen, mennesket og digteren* (*Andersen, the Man and the Writer*) in which a number of specialists made substantial contributions to the study of Andersen. Among the articles is an extremely informative investigation of the social conditions existing in Odense at the time Andersen was a child.

Recently, two psychologists, Eigil Nyborg and Arne Duuve,[21] a Dane and a Norwegian respectively, resumed the study of the relationship between Andersen and his fairy tales. Thus, their studies represent a return to the biographical method but on a new base. Primarily, they are interested in Andersen the man, and they use the tales to throw light upon his psyche. According to depth psychology the subconscious contains archetypal phenomena that in symbolic form appear in dreams and creative writing, and from the symbols that Andersen—presumably unconsciously—used in his tales these two psychologists are able to identify the mental conflicts and tensions that the writer struggled with throughout his life. His greatest problem had been his incomplete development to a male individual, a phenomenon due to the lack of a father-figure and to a severe mother-fixation entailing sexual fear and lifelong nervous disturbances. Thus the fairy tales are not regarded as works of art but as human documents; they are disguised messages from the deep layers of Andersen's soul. In this way the tales can also be taken as general symbols of human development.

Although Andersen's personal problems have long been known, this conclusion is helpful in understanding the subconscious motivation of his writing. Based on modern psychological principles, the two researchers have dealt exhaustively with these problems and have expressed them in the peculiar terminology of their science.

A third scholar, Peer E. Sørensen,[22] approaches Andersen from a Marxian perspective. Sørensen considers Andersen in relation to the development of bourgeois society and of modern capitalism in nineteenth-century Denmark and emphasizes the fairy-tale writer's difficult social position. Andersen came from the working class but wanted to be—and became—part of the bourgeoisie. He wanted to—and had to—acquire bourgeois breeding, but at the same time, with his working-class experience, he was critical of it. Andersen never managed to recognize this conflict—and it would be unreasonable to expect such recognition at that stage of social development—but it haunted his subconscious. His distressing feeling of insecurity in the bourgeois milieu was, according to Sørensen, the only reason for his nervousness. Another consequence of his social position was the hazy philosophy of the fairy tales; they do not face up to the fundamental problem of rich and poor. Furthermore, the fairy tales reflect the crisis in the bourgeois society. A tale such as "The Shadow," for example, shows pitilessly the meeting between bourgeois romantic breeding and modern capitalism.

Additionally, mention must be made of Niels Kofoed's doctoral dissertation,[23] in which Andersen's style, compositional and narrative techniques, artistic philosophy, and many other issues are discussed in depth. A number of structuralistic analyses of individual tales have also been published.[24] An extremely comprehensive biography, including an account of the tales, was published in English in 1975 by Elias Bredsdorff. The greatest contribution in the past decade to research on Andersen, apart from the publication of the diaries, however, is the multivolume text-critical edition of all the fairy tales under the editorship of Erik Dal, who now—after the death of H. Topsøe-Jensen—is the leading expert in the field of Andersen studies.

CHAPTER 5

Epilogue

THOSE Americans who visit Denmark naturally want to visit the places where Andersen lived, and to see the various monuments erected to his memory. In the town of his birth there is no birthplace to visit simply because nobody knows where he was born. But the pretty little house in which he spent his childhood still exists, although unfortunately it is surrounded by drab buildings from a later date. Also in Odense there is the extensive Hans Christian Andersen Museum. The way to the museum is the old Hans Jensen-Stræde, which, with its cobble-stones and little low houses, presents a charming old-fashioned street setting. Regrettably, this setting has partially been ruined by the ill-considered siting of an expressway through the old part of the town. The museum itself is housed in one of the old buildings and extends into a modern annex. Originally it was thought that the writer had been brought into the world in this house. Mementoes from Andersen's life have been collected here; such things as his school mark books, some of his letters and manuscripts, first editions of his works, as well as his drawings and cuttings. His ability at drawing was not inconsiderable, particularly when we take into account that he was quite untrained, while his paper-cuttings are masterpieces of their kind.[1] Finally, some of his possessions are here, among them the bed that after much fuss Andersen had to buy in 1866, his faithful trunk, and the rope that the ever fearful poet in his later days always took with him in case a fire broke out in his hotel, so that he would be able to climb down from his window.

In Copenhagen there is his grave in Assistens Cemetery, and there are two statues of him, one in the old park around Rosenborg Castle and the other on the Town Hall Square at the edge of the very busy, broad "H. C. Andersens Boulevard." Moreover, all tourists visit "Langelinie," the most pleasant part of Copenhagen's harbor, to see the world-famous statue called the Little Mermaid. A stone slab set in the wall of an attractive old house at Nyhavn Canal not far from the Royal Theatre indicates that Andersen lived in that house between 1834 and 1838 and also wrote his first fairy tales there. Unfortunately, it is not possible to visit the little attic room in which he lodged during his first years as a poet and a writer.

The best way of sensing Andersen's world is to be gained by strolling through the old streets of inner Copenhagen. This is the milieu he frequented often and it was here, after all, that he felt most at home. The atmosphere of these surroundings permeates many of his fairy tales.

The visitor should not fail to observe the Danish landscape. Some years ago the author of this book received a visit from two young college friends from the United States. Together we went on a trip to North Zealand and paid a visit, like most tourists, to two royal castles, Kronborg and Frederiksborg; but what caught the students' attention most of all was the summer landscape of Zealand with its graceful lines, delicate colors, and the gentle afternoon light. To them this experience provided the best background to Andersen's fairy tales, which often use the Danish landscape in the narrative. "How lovely it was out in the country . . ." is the opening of "The Ugly Duckling."

Finally, perhaps the alert visitor will be able to acquire one further link with the works of the fairy-tale writer: a feeling of the Danish character. In 1954 the English writer Rumer Godden visited Denmark while she was in the process of writing a description of Andersen's life. She had visited many countries throughout the world and claimed that after a short time in a country she was always able to form a fairly clear impression of what could be called the fundamental qualities of the nation. In Denmark this was not the case. She could not fathom the Danes. Each time she thought she had something she found only that there was something more. There is much truth in this observation. The Danes are a strange nation. The skepticism of the peasant is in their blood, and it has been strengthened by their creative writers: first Ludvig Holberg and then many others. Theirs is a skepticism toward the world around them and toward themselves. They are afraid to express themselves seriously; or, more precisely, they do not believe in their own seriousness and guard themselves behind a playful facade. They are therefore fond of walking the line between seriousness and nonseriousness. People are often unable to tell whether the Danes mean what they say or are just joking. Often they mean both; they let both possibilities remain open. Occasionally, for the sake of variety, they say the opposite of what they mean but do so with a slight emphasis that enables the other person to sense the real opinion. This is why foreigners find it so difficult to fathom the Danes.

A sojourn in Danish surroundings is necessary before one can get used to this vacillating mode of expression. The visitor who is not overhasty will then have a chance to understand it, and will be better equipped to catch and comprehend the secret of Andersen's narrative art. Andersen was every inch a Dane, and his mode of expression was Danish; his intentions in his tales might be serious, but they are often hidden behind irony; or he might be in jest while pretending to be in earnest. His real meaning is something that the reader must find out for himself, and in this game lies the incomparable charm of the fairy tales.

Notes and References

ABBREVIATIONS

A&C	E. Collin. *H. C. Andersen og det Collinske Huus.* Copenhagen, 1882.
Anderseniana	The annual publication of Anderseniana. Copenhagen, 1933–.
B&A	H. C. Andersen. *Eventyr og Historier.* 5 vols. Critical edition with commentaries by Hans Brix and Anker Jensen. Copenhagen, 1943.
BEC	*H. C. Andersens Brevveksling med Edvard og Henriette Collin.* 5 vols. Copenhagen, 1933–1937
BfA	*Breve fra Hans Christian Andersen.* Edited by C. St. A. Bille and Nikolaj Bøgh. 2 vols. Copenhagen, 1878.
BHH	*H. C. Andersens Brevveksling med Henriette Hanck.* Anderseniana, Copenhagen 1941–1946.
BJC	*H. C. Andersens Brevveksling med Jonas Collin den Ældre og andre medlemmer af det Collinske Hus.* 3 vols. Copenhagen, 1945–1948.
Bredsdorff	Elias Bredsdorff. *H. C. Andersen og England.* Copenhagen, 1954.
Bredsdorff HCA	Elias Bredsdorff. *Hans Christian Andersen.* London, 1975.
Brix	Hans Brix. *H. C. Andersen og hans Eventyr.* 2d ed. Copenhagen, 1970.
BScudder	*H. C. Andersen og Horace E. Scudder.* Edited by Jean Hersholt with notes by Waldemar Westergaard and an afterword by H. Topsøe-Jensen. Copenhagen, 1948.
BtA	*Breve til Hans Christian Andersen.* Edited by C. St. A. Bille and Nikolaj Bøgh. Copenhagen, 1877.
Dagbøger	*H. C. Andersens Dagbøger 1825–75.* Published by Det danske Sprog- og Litteraturselskab under the editorship of Kåre Olsen and H. Topsøe-Jensen. 9 vols. Copenhagen, 1971–1976.
Eventyr	*H. C. Andersens Eventyr.* Critical edition based on the original volumes of fairy-tales with variants, edited by Erik

153

	Dal with commentaries by Erling Nielsen. 5 vols. Copenhagen, 1963–1967. Incomplete.
Helweg	Hjalmar Helweg. *H. C. Andersen, en psykiatrisk Studie.* Copenhagen, 1927.
Levnedsbog	*H. C. Andersens Levnedsbog 1805–31.* Edited by H. Topsøe-Jensen. Copenhagen, 1962.
MeE	H. C. Andersen. *Mit Livs Eventyr uden Digtning.* From the writer's manuscript, edited by H. Topsøe-Jensen. Copenhagen, 1942.
MLE	H. C. Andersen. *Mit Livs Eventyr.* Reedited edition of the text by H. Topsøe-Jensen. With notes by H. G. Olrik and the editor. 2 vols. Copenhagen, 1951.
Olrik	H. G. Olrik. *Hans Christian Andersen.* Copenhagen, 1945.
RD	H. C. Andersen. *Romerske Dagbøger.* Edited by Paul V. Rubow and Topsøe-Jensen. Copenhagen, 1947.
Reumert	Elith Reumert. *H. C. Andersen og det Melchiorske Hjem.* Copenhagen, 1924.
SS	H. C. Andersen. *Samlede Skrifter* 2d ed. 15 vols. Copenhagen, 1876–1880.
Stampe	Rigmor Stampe. *H. C. Andersen og hans nærmeste Omgang.* Copenhagen, 1918.
Sv. L	Svend Larsen. "Barndomsbyen." in *H. C. Andersen, Mennesket og Digteren.* Odense, 1955.

Chapter One

1. *MLE*, I, 36–37.
2. For the following, see *Sv.L; Levnedsbog*, pp. 21–51; *MLE*, I, 27–53.
3. *Brix*, pp. 16–17.
4. *Olrik*, p. 57.
5. *Ibid.*, p. 66ff.
6. *Ibid.*, pp. 24–25.
7. *MLE*, I, 28.
8. *Levnedsbog*, p. 27.
9. *MLE*, I, 29–30.
10. More about this in *Olrik* p. 93ff.; *Brix*, pp. 24–27; *Sv. L*, pp. 18–19.
11. *MLE*, I, 41.
12. *Ibid.*, I, 36.
13. *Levnedsbog*, pp. 43f.
14. *Ibid.*, p. 44.
15. *MLE*, I, 48.
16. *Ibid.*, I, 50.
17. *Levnedsbog*, pp. 27–28.
18. *Ibid.*, p. 49.
19. *Ibid.*, pp. 53–93; *MLE*, I, 54–78.

20. *MLE*, I, 55.
21. *Ibid.*, I, 56.
22. *Ibid.*, I, 73.
23. *Ibid.*
24. *MeE* p. 208.
25. *Levnedsbog*, p. 92.
26. *Ibid.*, pp. 95–170; *MLE*, I, 79–96. The course of Andersen's life can also be followed through the letters in *A&C* and *BJC*. For material about Meisling, see Kjeld Galster, *H . C . Andersen og hans Rektor* (Kolding, 1933).
27. *A&C*, p. 3.
28. Galster, pp. 60ff.; *A&C*, pp. 75–81.
29. *Levnedsbog*, pp. 171–208; *MLE* I, 96–129.
30. *Stampe*, pp. 14ff., 22, 32–33, 37, 52–54.
31. *Levnedsbog*, p. 195.
32. *SS*, VIII, 83.
33. *Levnedsbog*, pp. 209–25.
34. *MLE*, I, 249.
35. Cf. *A&C*, p. 171.
36. Cf. Topsøe-Jensen, *Mit eget Eventyr uden Digtning* (Copenhagen, 1940), pp. 166ff.
37. *BEC*, I, 104.
38. *MLE*, I, 130–94; *BEC*, I; *BHH*; *BfA*, I; Dagbøger.
39. *MLE*, I, 130.
40. *BEC*, I, 164.
41. *MLE*, I, 149–81; *RD*; Elisabeth Hude in *Anderseniana*, 1967; Rubow in *Rom og Danmark gennem Tiderne* (Copenhagen, 1937), II, 76–96.
42. *BEC*, I, 190.
43. *BfA*, I, 142.
44. *Ibid.*, I, 146.
45. *Ibid.*, I, 150.
46. *Ibid.*, I, 144.
47. *BEC*, I, 195.
48. *BJC*, I, 99f.
49. *BfA*, I, 173.
50. *A&C*, p. 220.
51. *BJC*, I, 100.
52. *BEC*, I, 201ff.; V, 51f.
53. Edvard Collin later admitted that this letter had been written in an impatient mood and in an unkind tone. *A&C*, p. 221. Cf. *BJC*, I, 109–10.
54. *BfA*, I, 197–98.
55. *Ibid.*, I, 200.
56. *BHH*, pp. 83–85.
57. *BfA*, I, 215.
58. *MLE*, I, 435.
59. *BfA*, I, 248.

60. See the letters from his return journey in *BfA*, I, 214ff.
61. *BfA*, I, 248, 251.
62. *Ibid.*, I, 224ff.
63. *Ibid.*, I, 228–29.
64. *MLE*; *A&C*; *BEC*, I; *BfA*, I–II; *BHH*.
65. Søren Kierkegaard, *Samlede værker* (Copenhagen 1962–1964), vol. 1.
66. *MLE*, I, 235–36; *A&C*, p. 328ff.
67. *BEC*, I, 316.
68. *MLE*; *BJC*, I–II; *BEC*, I–II; *BfA*, II.
69. *BJC*, I, 186.
70. *Ibid.*, I, 244.
71. Louis Bobe, *H. C. Andersen og Storhertug Carl Alexander* (Copenhagen, 1905); E. Jonas, *H. C. Andersens Briefwechsel mit dem Grossherzog Carl Alexander* (Leipzig, 1887).
72. *MLE*, I, 338–40, where it is said that they met later and on that occasion Grimm knew who Andersen was. *BJC*, I, 246–47.
73. *BEC*, II, 12–13.
74. *Ibid.*, II, 64.
75. For the following, see *Bredsdorff* (includes extensive documentation); *Bredsdorff HCA*, pp. 183–218, and the same author's *H. C. Andersen og Charles Dickens* (Copenhagen, 1951; English edition, Cambridge, 1956); *BJC*, II, 6ff.
76. *BfA*, II, 374.
77. *MLE*, I, 298.
78. *Ibid.*, I, 474, 295ff.
79. *Ibid.*, I, 475. On Andersen's almanac, see below chapter 3, note 15.
80. *Ibid.*, I, 300.
81. *MLE*, I, 340–41; compare H. Topsøe-Jensen; *Mit Livs Eventyr uden Digtning* (Copenhagen, 1940), p. 59.
82. *MLE*, II, 67ff.
83. *Ibid.*, II, 82ff.
84. *BEC*, II, 194.
85. *MLE*; *BEC*, II–IV; *BfA*, II.
86. *BfA*, II, 242.
87. *BEC*, II, 201.
88. *Stampe*, pp. 191–92.
89. *A&C*, p. 352.
90. *MLE*, II, 207, 447.
91. *A&C*, p. 432.
92. *MLE*, II, 339f.
93. *Ibid.*, II, 340–52.
94. *BEC*, III, 246.
95. *Ibid.*, II, 392; cf. Helweg, chap. 5.
96. For the following, see *Reumert*.

97.   *BEC*, IV, 240; V, 453.
98.   Arne Portman, *H . C. Andersens sidste Dage* (Copenhagen, 1952),
pp. 7ff.
99.   *Reumert*, pp. 224–26.
100. *Ibid.*, pp. 229–31.
101. Copenhagen Press, 11–12 August; copies are at the University
Library in Copenhagen.
102. Georg Brandes, "Essay on Søren Kierkegaard," in *Samlede Skrifter*
(Copenhagen, 1899–1902), II, 273.
103. *MLE*, I, 27.
104. *Stampe*, p. 189.
105. *BEC*, II, 261.
106. *BHH*, p. 199, 225, 315.
107. *BEC*, II, 14–15.
108. *Diary*, 8 December 1825, quoted in *A&C*, p. 91–92.

Chapter Two

1.   *A&C*, p. 476.
2.   *BJC*, I, 174; *BHH*, p. 350. See also Carl Fehrmann; *Diktaren och de
skapande ögonblicken* (Stockholm, 1974), pp. 54–58, 165.
3.   *BfA*, I, 368.
4.   *Ibid.*, II, 243.
5.   H. Topsøe-Jensen, in *Festskrift til Lis Jacobsen* (Copenhagen,
1952), and in *Fund og Forskning* (Copenhagen, 1962–1963).
6.   See above chapter 1, note 65.
7.   Kierkegaard, I, 29.
8.   *Ibid.*, I, 38.
9.   *SS*, IV, 109.
10. Kierkegaard, I, 54–55, 44–45.
11. *BHH*, 195.
12. The newspaper *Dagen*, 29 November 1837.
13. See *SS*, IV, 3–10, 91–94.
14. *Ibid.*, pp. 167–71.
15. *Ibid.*, pp. 292–93.
16. *B&B*, I, 368.
17. For more details, see Villy Sørensen; *Hverken-eller* (Copenhagen,
1961), pp. 136–57.
18. *BfA*, II, 335–36.
19. Chapter 7 (*SS*, VI, 74).
20. See bibliography.
21. *A&C*, 111.
22. *Ibid.*, 305–8.
23. Johanne Luise Heiberg, *Et Liv genoplevet i Erindringen*, 5th ed.,
(Copenhagen, 1973), I, 318–36.

24.   *MLE*, I, 226.
25.   *Ibid.*, I, 446.
26.   *Eventyr af H . C . Andersen, Verdensudgave* (Copenhagen, 1900), p. viii.
27.   From Andersen, *Seven Poems*, trans. R. P. Keigwin (Odense, 1955). With the exception of the poems on pages 80 and 82—translated by Douglas Holmes—all translations of poetry in this chapter are by Keigwin.
28.   *Stampe*, pp. 84–85.
29.   *MLE*, I, 94, 405–6.
30.   *Ibid.*, I, 301.
31.   *Olrik*, p. 202.
32.   *A&C*, p. 459.
33.   H. Topsøe-Jensen; *H . C . Andersen og andre Studier* (Odense, 1966), p. 120.

Chapter Three

1.   Quoted in *B&A*, V, 381.
2.   *BHH*, p. 104; *BfA*, I, 292.
3.   *A&C*, pp. 495–96.
4.   Paul V. Rubow; *H . C . Andersens Eventyr* (Copenhagen, 1927), p. 173f. (3d ed. 1967, p. 179ff.); Bo Grønbech; *H . C . Andersens Eventyrverden* (Copenhagen, 1945), p. 136ff. (2d ed. 1964, p. 108f.); *Eventyr*, I, 189.
5.   *A&C*, pp. 259–62.
6.   *BfA*, I, 315, 283, 366.
7.   *Ibid.*, I, 306; *MLE*, I, 289.
8.   For the following, see Andersen's own comments on "Fairy tales and Stories," 1862 and 1874. *SS*, XV, 297ff. (also printed in *B&A*, V, 384ff.).
9.   *BfA*, II, 94; *MLE*, I, 290.
10.   Foreword to *Eventyr fortalte for Børn*, vol. 3 (1837); reprinted in *B&A*, V, 382.
11.   *MLE*, II, 157.
12.   *SS*, XV, 299 (also *B&A*, V, 387).
13.   For the following, see Bo Grønbech, pp. 167–71 (2d ed., pp. 133–37).
14.   *BfA*, II, 106.
15.   Andersen's daily notes for 11–12 October 1843 (*B&A*, II, 379). When Andersen was in Copenhagen he only jotted notes in his almanac. This is now to be found in the Royal Library in Copenhagen and has not been published. The diaries proper were kept up during his journeys and in later years also in Copenhagen.
16.   The idea for this tale was taken from an Arabian proverb that Charles Dickens had brought to Andersen's notice: "When the Emperor's horse was given gold shoes the Dung-Beetle also put out its leg" (*SS*, XV, 309).
17.   *MLE*, I, 486–87.
18.   For the following, see Bo Grønbech, chap. 10 (2d ed., chap. 9).

19. See Peer E. Sørensen, *H. C. Andersen og Herskabet: Studier i borgerlig krisebevidsthed* (Århus, 1973), p. 195.

20. *MLE*, I, 50.

21. For the following, see Bo Grønbech, "Eventyrenes Filosofi," in *H. C. Andersen, Mennesket og Digteren* (Odense, 1955).

22. This fairy tale was inspired by Adalbert von Chamisso's tale *Peter Schlemihls wundersame Geschichte* (1814), the story of a man who sold his shadow to the Devil, and by Andersen's observations of his own shadow.

23. *BfA*, II, 95.

24. *Brix*, pp. 165–67.

Chapter Four

1. *Fædrelandet*, 18 December 1852.

2. *BtA*, p. 245.

3. *Dansk Maanedsskrift*, April 1855; *Nordisk Tidsskrift for Litteratur og Kunst*, 1, no. 3 (1863), 499ff.

4. Georg Brandes; *Samlede Skrifter* (Copenhagen, 1899–1902). II, p 91ff. The citation: pp. 92–93.

5. For the following, see *Bredsdorff*, pp. 428–85, particularly pp. 438–47, 457–58, 476–78, 480; summing up on pp. 484–85. For English writers' opinions of Andersen's fairy tales see Bredsdorff, in *Anderseniana* (1956), pp. 325–51.

6. For the following, see *BScudder*.

7. *BJC*, I, 318.

8. Diary for 1 April 1862.

9. *BScudder*, p. 48.

10. *Bredsdorff HCA*, pp. 333–36, and, more detailed, *Bredsdorff* pp. 489–521.

11. Erik Dal, "Hans Christian Andersen's Tales and America," *Scandinavian Studies*, 40, no. 1 (February 1968), 1–25.

12. *Bredsdorff HCA*, pp. 336–37.

13. Cf. *Anderseniana* (1970), pp. 74ff. (with very pertinent observations about a translator's difficulties).

14. Hans Christian Andersen, *The Story of a Mother in fifteen Languages*, ed. Jean Pio and Vilh. Thomsen (London, 1875).

15. *Une mère: Conte de Hans Christian Andersen en vingt-deux langues*, ed. P. Em. Hansen (St. Petersburg, 1894).

16. *H. C. Andersen: Kejserens nye Klæder paa femogtyve Sprog*, ed. Louis Hjelmslev and Axel Sandal (Copenhagen, 1944).

17. A bibliography of translations of Andersen's fairy tales (by Juel Møller) is accessible at the Royal Library in Copenhagen.

18. *SS*, XV, 302.

19. *Samlet Oversigt over arrangementerne i udlandet i anledning af H. C. Andersens 150-årsdag, 2 April 1955* (Copenhagen). In this connection

may be mentioned *H. C. Andersen, Klip fra udenlandsk presse i 100-året for digterens død* (Copenhagen, 1975).
20. The reader is referred to the bibliography.
21. Eigil Nyborg, *Den indre linje i H. C. Andersens eventyr: En psykologisk studie* (Copenhagen, 1962); Arne Duve, *Symbolikken i H. C. Andersens eventyr* (Oslo, 1967).
22. See chapter 3, note 19.
23. Niels Kofoed, *Studier i H. C. Andersens fortællekunst* (Copenhagen, 1967).
24. For example, Søren Baggesen, "Individuation eller frelse? Om slutningen af H. C. Andersens eventyr 'Den lille Havfrue,' " *Kritik* (Copenhagen), no. 1 (1967); Erik A. Nielsen, "Blandt luftens ånder," *Meddelelser fra Dansklærerforeningen*, no. 2 (1971).

Chapter Five

1. Most of Andersen's drawings originate from his travels in his early years. See Kjeld Heltoft, *H. C. Andersens Billedkunst* (Copenhagen, 1969), and *H. C. Andersens Tegninger til Otto Zinck*, 2 vols. (Odense, 1972). His paper cuttings were made when he wished to amuse the children in the homes of his friends. See Poul Uttenreiter, *H. C. Andersens Billedbog* (Copenhagen, 1944).

Selected Bibliography

PRIMARY SOURCES

1. Collected Works

Samlede Skrifter. 15 vols. 2d ed. Copenhagen, 1876–1880.

2. Editions of the Tales

Eventyr og Historier. 5 vols. Copenhagen, 1943. With notes and commentaries by Hans Brix and Anker Jensen.
Eventyr. Edited by Erik Dal and Erling Nielsen. Copenhagen, 1963–. Critical edition based on the original fairy tales and variants. By 1977 five volumes had been published.

3. English translations of the Tales

It's perfectly true and other stories by Hans Christian Andersen, trans. by Paul Leyssac, New York, 1938; *The Complete Andersen*, trans. by Jean Hersholt, New York, 1947; *80 Fairy Tales* by Hans Christian Andersen, trans. by R. P. Keigwin, Odense, 1951–1960; *Hans Christian Andersen Fairy Tales and Stories*, trans. by Reginald Spink, London and New York, 1960.
Tales the Moon Can Tell. Translated by R. P. Keigwin. Copenhagen, 1955.

4. Novels and Travel Books

Romaner og Rejseskildringer. Edited by H. Topsøe-Jensen. 7 vols. Copenhagen, 1941–1944.

a. Novels
Improvisatoren. Copenhagen, 1835. English edition: *The Improvisatore, or, Life in Italy.* Translated by Mary Howitt. 2 vols. London, 1845.
O.T. Copenhagen. 1836. English edition: see next entry.
Kun en Spillemand. Copenhagen, 1837. English edition: *Only a Fiddler! and O.T., or Life in Denmark.* Translated by Mary Howitt. 2 vols. London, 1845.

De to Baronesser. Copenhagen, 1848. English edition: *The Two Baronesses.* Translated by Charles Beckwith. 2 vols. London, 1848.
At være eller ikke være. Copenhagen, 1857. English edition: *To Be, or Not to Be?* Translated by Mrs. Bushby. London, 1857.
Lykke-Peer. Copenhagen, 1870. English edition: *Lucky Peer.* Translated by Horace E. Scudder. *Scribner's Monthly* (January, February, March, and April 1871).

b. Travel Books

Skyggebilleder af en Reise til Harzen, det sachsiske Schweitz etc. etc. i Sommeren 1831. Copenhagen, 1831. English edition: *Rambles in the Romantic Regions of the Hartz Mountains, Saxon Switzerland.* Translated by Charles Beckwith. London, 1848.
En Digters Bazar. Copenhagen, 1842. English edition: *A Poet's Bazaar.* Translated by Charles Beckwith. London, 1846; also: *A Poet's Bazaar, Pictures of Travel in Germany, Italy, Greece and the Orient.* New York, 1871.
I Sverige. Copenhagen, 1851. English edition: *Pictures of Travel in Sweden: Among the Hartz Mountains, and in Switzerland with A Visit at Charles Dicken's House.* New York, 1871.
I Spanien. Copenhagen, 1863. English edition: *A Visit to Spain.* Translated, edited, and introduced by Grace Thornton. London, 1975.
Et Besøg i Portugal 1866. Copenhagen, 1868. English edition: *A Visit to Portugal 1866.* Translated, with an introduction, notes, and appendixes by Grace Thornton. London, 1972.

5.   Poems

Hans Christian Andersen: Seven Poems. Translated by R. P. Keigwin. Odense, 1955.

6.   Autobiographies

H. C. Andersens Levnedsbog 1805–1831. Edited by H. Topsøe-Jensen. Copenhagen, 1962. Andersen's first large autobiography, written for his friends 1832. The manuscript was long presumed lost but was found and first published in 1926 by Hans Brix. This work has not been translated into English.
Das Märchen meines Lebens ohne Dichtung. 2 vols. Leipzig, 1847. Edited from Andersen's Danish manuscript, with commentaries, by H. Topsøe-Jensen under the title *Mit eget Eventyr uden Digtning* (Copenhagen, 1942). English edition: *The True Story of My Life.* Translated from the German by Mary Howitt. London, 1847.
Mit Livs Eventyr. Copenhagen, 1855. English edition: *The Story of My Life.* Translated by Horace E. Scudder. New York, 1871. With additional

chapters covering the years 1855–1867. Recently issued in a revised edition by H. Topsøe-Jensen, with notes by H. G. Olrik and the editor (Copenhagen, 1951). This edition includes the additional chapters first published in Scudder's translation. A new English edition appeared in 1954: *The Fairy-Tale of My Life*. Translated by W. Glyn Jones. Copenhagen, 1954.

7. Correspondence

The Andersen-Scudder Letters. Berkeley, 1949. Hans Christian Andersen's correspondence with Horace Elisha Scudder. Notes and translation by Waldemar Westergaard.

H . C . Andersen og Henriette Wulff. En Brevveksling. Edited by H. Topsøe-Jensen. 3 vols. Copenhagen, 1959–1960.

8. English Translations

It's Perfectly True And Other Stories by Hans Christian Andersen, trans. by Paul Leyssac. New York, 1938.

The Complete Andersen, trans. by Jean Hersholt. New York, 1947.

80 Fairy Tales by Hans Christian Andersen, trans by R. P. Keigwin. Odense, 1951–1960.

Hans Christian Andersen *Fairy Tales*, trans. by Reginald Spink. London and New York, 1960.

Tales the Moon Can Tell (Picture Book Without Pictures). Trans. by R. P. Keigwin. Copenhagen, 1955.

The Improvisatore, or Life in Italy. Trans. by Mary Howitt. 2 vols. London, 1845.

Only a Fiddler! and O.T., or Life in Denmark. Trans. by Mary Howitt. 2 vols. London, 1845.

The Two Baronesses. Trans. by Charles Beckwith. 2 vols. London, 1848.

To Be, or Not to Be? Trans. by Mrs. Bushby. London, 1857.

Lucky Peer. Trans. by Horace E. Scudder. *Scribner's Monthly*. January, February, March, and April, 1871.

Rambles in the Romantic Regions of the Hartz Mountains, Saxon Switzerland. Trans. by Charles Beckwith. London, 1848.

A Poet's Bazaar. 3 vols.. Trans. by Charles Beckwith. London, 1846.

A Poet's Bazaar, Pictures of Travel in Germany, Italy, Greece and the Orient. New York, 1871.

Pictures of Travel: In Sweden, Among the Hartz Mountains, and in Switzerland, with a Visit at Charles Dickens' House. New York, 1871.

A Visit to Spain. Translated, edited, and introduced by Grace Thornton. London, 1975.

A Visit to Portugal 1866. Translated, with an introduction, notes and appendixes by Grace Thornton. London, 1972.

Hans Christian Andersen: Seven Poems. Trans. by R. P. Keigwin. Odense, 1955.
The True Story of My Life. Trans. from the German by Mary Howitt. London, 1847.
The Story of My Life. Trans. by Horace E. Scudder. New York, 1871.
The Fairy-Tale of My Life. Trans. by W. Glyn Jones. Copenhagen, 1954.
The Andersen-Scudder Letters. Notes and translation by Waldemar Westergaard. Berkeley, 1949.

SECONDARY SOURCES

1. Bibliographies.

BREDSDORFF, ELIAS: *Danish Literature in English Translation.* Copenhagen: Munksgaard, 1950. With a special Hans Christian Andersen supplement. A bibliography.
—————: *A Critical Guide to the Literature on Hans Christian Andersen.* In *Scandinavica*, 6, no. 1 (May 1967) Academic Press, London & New York.
—————: *Hans Christian Andersen: A Bibliographical Guide to His Works.* In *Scandinavica* ibid.
JØRGENSEN, AAGE: *H. C. Andersen Litteraturen 1875–1968.* Aarhus. Akademisk Boghandel, 1970. Works about H. C. Andersen.
NIELSEN, BIRGER FRANK: *H. C. Andersen Bibliografi.* Hagerup: Copenhagen, 1942. Andersen's Danish works 1822–1875.

2. Books and Articles.

BOBÉ, LOUIS: *H. C. Andersen og Storhertug Carl Alexander af Sachsen-Weimar-Eisenach.* Copenhagen: Hagerup, 1905.
BRANDES, EDVARD: "H. C. Andersen: Personlighed og Værk". In *Litterære Tendenser.* Copenhagen: Gyldendal, 1968.
BRANDES, GEORG: *H. C. Andersen som Eventyrdigter.* Samlede Skrifter II, pp. 91–132. Copenhagen: Gyldendal, 1899. See page 135 of the present work.
—————: *H. C. Andersen som Menneske og Eventyrdigter.* Copenhagen: Det nordiske Forlag, 1900. A brilliant description of Andersen, whom Brandes knew personally, and of his narrative art.
BREDSDORFF, ELIAS: *H. C. Andersen og Charles Dickens.* Copenhagen: Rosenkilde og Bagger, 1951. English edition: Cambridge: W. Heffer & Sons, 1956.
—————: *H. C. Andersen og England.* Copenhagen: Rosenkilde og Bagger, 1954.
—————: *Hans Christian Andersen: the Story of his Life and Work,* London:

Phaidon, 1975. A broad description with extensive quotations from letters and similar documents.

BRIX, HANS: *H. C. Andersen og hans Eventyr*. 2d ed. Copenhagen: Gyldendal, 1970. A genetic-biographical approach to the fairy-tales (see page 145 of the present work). This book must be used with caution as several of its hypotheses have proven to be invalid.

CHRISTENSEN, GEORG: "H. C. Andersen og de danske Folkeeventyr." In *Danske Studier*, Copenhagen: Gyldendal, 1906.

COLLIN, EDVARD: *H. C. Andersen og det Collinske Huus*. Copenhagen: Reitzel, 1882. An important work for Andersen students. Depicts Andersen's life and personality, mainly through his letters, which have, however, been arbitrarily shortened. The final part of the book is about the Collin family.

DAL, ERIK: "Hans Christian Andersen's Tales and America." *Scandinavian Studies*, 40, no. 1 (February, 1968).

————: "Introduction". In *H. C. Andersens Samlede Eventyr og Historier*. Commemorative edition. Copenhagen: Lademann, 1975. Discusses Andersen's use of fairy-tale style and the various types of fairy tales in his total production, as well as the Danish illustrations of the tales.

GALSTER, KJELD: *H. C. Andersen og hans Rektor*. Kolding: Konrad Jørgensen, 1933. A thorough, well-documented investigation of Andersen's school period.

GARDE, ANNELISE: *H. C. Andersen og hans kreds*. Copenhagen: Arnold Busck, 1967. A number of fine characterizations of Andersen and his friends based on an analysis of their handwriting.

GODDEN, RUMER: *Hans Christian Andersen*. New York: Alfred A. Knopf, 1955. A readable description of Andersen's life with comments on his tales.

GRØNBECH, BO: *H. C. Andersen's Eventyrverden*. Copenhagen: Povl Branner, 1945; 2nd (slightly shortened) ed., Copenhagen: Reitzel, 1964. A study of the distinctiveness of Andersen's fairy-tale world with regard to setting, characters, and narration.

————: "Eventyrenes Filosofi." In *H. C. Andersen, Mennesket og Digteren*. Odense: Flensted 1955 pp. 194–207.

————: *H. C. Andersen, levnedsløb, digtning, personlighed*. Copenhagen: Arnold Busck, 1971. A comprehensive picture of the writer and his work.

H.C. Andersen, Mennesket og Digteren. Odense: Flensted, 1955. Contains essays about Andersen's native town of Odense, Funen, the fairy tales, Andersen's relations to other Scandinavians and to England, and much more.

HELWEG, HJALMAR: *H.C. Andersen, en psykiatrisk Studie*. Copenhagen: Hagerup, 1927. For further details see p. 145.

HOLBECK, H.ST.: *H.C. Andersens Religion*. Copenhagen: Schønberg, 1947.

JACOBSEN, H.H.: *H.C. Andersen på Fyn*. Odense: Skandinavisk Bogforlag, 1968.

JONAS, E.: *H.C. Andersens Briefwechsel mit dem Grossherzog Carl Alexander*. Leipzig: Wilhelm Friedrich, 1887.

MARKER, FREDERICK J.: *Hans Christian Andersen and the Romantic Theatre*. Toronto: University of Toronto Press, 1971. Evaluates Andersen as a dramatist in the new spirit of Romanticism.

NYGAARD, GEORG: *H.C. Andersen og København*. Copenhagen: Foreningen Fremtiden, 1938. A lively description of Andersen's time in the Danish capital.

PORTMAN, ARNE: *H.C. Andersens sidste dage*. Copenhagen: Preben Witt, 1952. The author, a doctor, claims convincingly that Andersen's final illness was sclerosis and not liver cancer.

REUMERT, ELITH: *H.C. Andersen og det Melchiorske Hjem*. Copenhagen: Hagerup, 1924. A picture of the poet's life in later years.

————: *H.C. Andersen som han var*. Copenhagen: Hagerup, 1925. English edition: *Hans Andersen the man*. Trans. by Jessie Bröchner. London: Methuen & Co. 1927. A characterization of Andersen's personality.

RUBOW, PAUL V.: *H.C. Andersens Eventyr, Forhistorien, ide og form, sprog og stil*. 3rd ed. Copenhagen: Gyldendal, 1967. For further details see p. 146.

————: "H.C. Andersens Pariserreiser". In *Danske i Paris gennem Tiderne*. Copenhagen: Reitzel, 1936.

————: "Danske Guldalderforfattere i Rom." In *Rom og Danmark gennem Tiderne*. Vol. 2. Copenhagen: Levin & Munksgaard, 1937.

RUE, HARALD: "H.C. Andersen". In *Litteratur og Samfund*. Copenhagen: Fischer, 1937. An account of the poet's social position and its importance to his works.

SCHMITZ, V.A.: *H.C. Andersens Märchendichtung*. Greifswald: L. Bamberg, 1925. Discusses the same problems as Rubow in his *H.C. Andersens Eventyr*, only less extensively.

SØRENSEN, VILLY: "De djævelske traumer". In *Hverken-eller, kritiske betragtninger* Copenhagen: Gyldendal, 1961. See pp. 69–70 and n. 17.

SPINK, REGINALD: *Hans Christian Andersen and his world*. London: Everyman, 1972. A brief biography illustrated by his works.

STAMPE, RIGMOR: *H.C. Andersen og hans nærmeste Omgang*. Copenhagen: Aschehoug, 1918. A picture of the Collins family and at the same time an excellent description of the Copenhagen milieu. See p. 57.

SVANHOLM, CHR.: *H.C. Andersens Ungdoms-tro*. Trondheim: Theim, 1952. A thorough depiction of Andersen's Christian faith until 1828.

TOPSØE-JENSEN, H.: *Mit eget Eventyr uden Digtning: En Studie over H.C. Andersen som Selvbiograf*. Copenhagen: Gyldendal, 1940. An account of the writer's work with his autobiographies and of their credibility. See pp. 56 and 145.

_____: *Omkring Levnedsbogen: En Studie over H.C. Andersen som Selvbiograf 1820–45*. Copenhagen: Gyldendal, 1943. An account of the origin of *Levnedsbogen* and Andersen's other and shorter biographical sketches.

_____: "H.C. Andersen og USA". In *Anderseniana 1949*. Odense: 1949.

_____: "H.C. Andersens Religion". In *Anderseniana 1963*. Odense: 1963.

_____: *H.C. Andersen og andre Studier*. Fwaske Studier VI. Odense Bys Museer, 1966. Mostly reprints of articles.

_____: *Buket til Andersen. Bemærkninger til 25 Eventyr*. Copenhagen: Gad, 1971. A goldmine of information about the fairy tales.

Un livre sur le poète danois Hans Christian Andersen, sa vie et son oeuvre. Copenhagen: Berlingske Bogtrykkeri, 1955. Contains essays on Andersen's life, the fairy tales, and their translations, and his significance for posterity.

VEDEL, VALDEMAR: "H.C. Andersens Eventyr". In *Tilskueren*. Copenhagen: Gyldendal, 1926. An account of the literary background of Andersen's fairy tales.

Index

168